DR. ROHIT VASANT KALE

ISBN
Paperback 979-8-89632-721-9
Hardcase 979-8-89699-328-5

"In questions of science, the authority of a thousand is not worth the humble reasoning of a single individual."

-Galileo Galilei

Acknowledgements

This book is dedicated to my parents, Vasant Kale and Nilima Kale. It would not have been possible without their constant support and motivation. They not only provided emotional encouragement but also created an environment where spirituality could flourish and have an important place in my heart. My mother went above and beyond by recording many chapters from spiritual books in her own voice, which made complex concepts about the Trideva and the Bhagavad Gita clearer in my mind. I still listen to her recordings often and continue to gain valuable insights from them. I am forever indebted to them for shaping me into the person I am today.

I am also deeply grateful to my sister, Dr. Meenal, for taking extra care of my parents during their illnesses, allowing me to focus on my work without worry. I owe a debt of gratitude to my uncle, Mukund Kaka, for his efforts in helping our family understand the intricacies of the Bhagavad Gita, a contribution that continues to resonate with us today. I am also thankful to my entire family for creating a supportive environment that has been essential to my journey. I am especially grateful to my elder cousin, Chetan Dada, for his constant motivation as I developed the theory of DGR.

I want to thank my sons, Tanay and Srihan, whose daily hugs lifted my spirits and brightened my day, especially as I wrestled with the frustrations of difficult Physics concepts while developing the theory. Their love was a constant source of strength, especially during the challenging moments when I faced rejection from over six reputed journals in my attempts to publish the theory in mainstream Physics literature. I am also thankful to my wife Puja, whose sacrifices and support were crucial without which I wouldn't be able to complete this book or would have had to abandon it prematurely before completion.

I am deeply indebted to Shri Dr. Shrikrishna Deshmukh, affectionately known as Deshmukh Kaka or Doctor Kaka, my guru, for guiding me toward spiritual awakening. His teachings have been instrumental in the creation of this book. I am also particularly grateful to Shri Pramod Walvekar for his valuable contribution to the book.

I could not have reached this point without the guidance of all my teachers, including the Physics educators who shared their knowledge selflessly. They shaped my thoughts, illuminated the path of learning, and helped dispel the mist of ignorance from my mind.

I acknowledge the use of Chat GPT and Grammarly AI for improving the flow of English and checking for grammatical errors at selected paragraphs of the book. I am also grateful to the websites from which I could acquire the Sanskrit Shlokas and learned their significance and inferences in English (including Stotra.in, holy-bhagavad-gita.org, shlokam.org, vedicfeed.com, isha.sadhguru.org, greenmesg.org and sanskritforus.com) as references to the commonly held beliefs about the Trideva and I thank all these websites for the same.

I extend my heartfelt gratitude to the publishers and everyone involved in the successful completion of this book. Your contributions have made its publication possible and allowed it to reach readers far and wide.

This book is a tribute to my paternal grandfather, late Madhav Pralhad Kale, who sparked my curiosity about Shiva and emphasized the significance of faith in the Trideva. I remain deeply thankful to him and to my paternal grandmother, late Nalini Madhav Kale, for teaching me the *Rama Raksha Stotra* and nurturing my love for Prabhu Shri Ram.

I also express my sincere gratitude to my maternal grandparents, late Dr Shankar Bhagwant Thombre and late Kamal Shankar Thombre, for lovingly caring for me and my sister during our formative years. Their guidance helped shape our beliefs and instilled in us a deep sense of love and gratitude.

I thank you, the reader, to have the faith and willingness to read my work and have the curiosity to know more about the Trideva.

Lastly, I thank the Almighty for entrusting me with this work and deeming me worthy of it. I am profoundly grateful for the countless blessings bestowed upon me.

Contents

Introduction

The Book

Being a Hindu by birth, I was cognisant of many commonly held beliefs and Puranic tales.

From childhood, Sanatani Hindus are introduced to numerous Vedic teachings. With the rise of scientific thinking and the influence of the English language, many of these beliefs may start to appear orthodox and unscientific. However, the significance of the Trideva in a typical Hindu household, culture, and festivals should not be underestimated. One of the principal teachings that a young Hindu child is taught about is the three principal deities in Sanatan Dharma. Puranic literature and also the Bhagavad Gita teaches about the three Gunas namely Rajas, Tamas and Sattva. The extremely complex scientific theory that describes the most fundamental aspects of creation (a theory of everything) was possibly the last place one would expect to find the Trideva. What this book is and what it is not is described subsequently.

But this book is an attempt to understand the Trideva from a scientific point of view with an open mind towards the teachings of the Vedas.

It all began with my third book, in which, in an attempt to answer some of the most profound questions posed by today's physicists, I came across a theory first described by Einstein. This theory can be considered a cousin of General Relativity. I endeavoured to develop it into a full-fledged theory of Quantum Gravity and a potential Theory of Everything. The theory, which I called ***Dynamic General Relativity (DGR),*** naturally reiterated many aspects of the Trideva without much effort.

Although complex, a deep understanding of this theory is not necessary to grasp the connection between it and the Trideva. While the theory is still in its infancy, it shows great promise.

The relationship between the Trideva and this theory could shed light on the truth behind various beliefs associated with the Trideva. Furthermore, these striking coincidences could provide the much-needed motivation to reconsider the teachings of the Vedas—not as myths, but as potential sources of profound insight. At the same time, this approach might encourage us to think outside the box and pursue the necessary lines of inquiry to address the enigmatic questions facing modern physics, as opposed to the prevailing attitude of "Shut up and calculate.

What are the intentions of writing this book?

The only intention is to document the possible similarities between the Vedic description of the Trideva and the description of the theory of DGR. In a way, the book intends to understand the Trideva and their real meaning. In a way, the book aims to understand the deep hidden meaning within Physics. There is an intention to give a new direction to the current Fundamentals of Physics. Another important purpose is to make people aware of the extremely scientific nature of the Vedas and to take them seriously and understand them instead of considering them as "Superstition" or "Myth" as is widely portrayed.

Who should read this book?

- Any Sanatani Hindu who intends to know the Trideva and come closer to them should read the book.
- Any Sanatani Hindu who has a basic education with some knowledge of basic physics and has a curiosity to know what the commonly told things about the Trideva might potentially mean.
- Any person who has a background of Science or Physics and has curiosity to know what the Unified Theory of Everything might look like and what is its relationship with the Vedic teachings and the Trideva.
- Any individual with the intention to do research on Quantum Gravity and Unified Theory of Everything
- Those who are curious about questions like what energy is, what light is, what gravity is, and how it works.

Why is this book needed?

- This book is basically aimed at documenting the extreme coincidences that were found while developing the theory of DGR.
- It was observed that the DGR theory essentially reflects the Vedic teachings of the Trideva, including their attire and qualities.

- This book has no intention to teach Vedas or Other Puranic literature since I am no expert in it. One of the definite intentions is to take the Vedic teachings more seriously. The author recommends more research on such teachings from the Vedas and their potential alternate explanations.
- One has to note that this book can only deal with some of the Vedic sayings and beliefs. Thus, the possibility of selection bias cannot be ruled out. This means that the book selectively focuses on those aspects of the Trideva which coincide with the Theory and disregards those that do not match.
- The similarities observed between the Trideva in Vedic and Puranic teachings may be coincidences and could potentially be inaccurate. Even the theory of DGR lacks concrete proof and remains speculative. Therefore, the views expressed can be considered the author's opinion, and while they are intriguing, there is a possibility that they may be incorrect.
- It is clear that the similarities cannot be brushed under the carpet as "just co-incidences" and there is no way that the ancient Vedic/Puranic authors or teachers knew anything close to a Theory of Everything in Fundamentals of Physics. One or two things coinciding with the ancient Vedic teachings could as well be due to coincidence, but almost 20 similarities are too much to come just by chance in my opinion.
- Although mathematical rigour is awaited yet, even the theory of DGR is more versatile than General Relativity and Quantum Mechanics taken alone and in my opinion

is more valid than both of them. This is because GR can be proven wrong by performing "the double slit experiment" while QM can be proven wrong by Gravitational lensing, while both of these can be successfully explained by DGR. I think the Physicists of the West have extreme bias against attempting to understand DGR probably due to the Stereotype of the author being "a non-physicist and an Indian". However Indian Physicists should take up the task of understanding the theory and conducting more research on its validity. The author being a "non-professional" can take the theory only up to a certain level of complexity. At some point, professional physicists have to acknowledge their mistakes in GR or QM and take over DGR. Indeed, this can be a major step in further advancements in Fundamentals of Physics.

Prerequisites to understand before reading this book

- This book requires a basic understanding of physics. While the theories are not presented in great detail and are straightforward enough for even children to grasp, a genuine interest and conceptual knowledge of physics is essential to fully appreciate the content.
- The theory described is not yet an accepted scientific theory, and further work is required. However, the hurdles in making it acceptable to the scientific community are more psychological.

What this book is not

- This book has no intention to promote any religious belief and is purely a scientific endeavour to analyse one's beliefs.
- This book is not a book that teaches Vedic teachings or Spirituality as I am not trained enough in that to do the same.
- This book does not intend to give the theory of Dynamic General Relativity in detail.
- Although developing some understanding of "what the theory of DGR is?", is a prerequisite to comprehending this book, a detailed knowledge of DGR is not needed. Thus, even those not having any physics or science background can grasp the theory and this book.
- This book has no intention to teach physics.
- **The book has no intention to prove one deity superior to another and there is no intention to hurt the sentiments of any community or group of people. If any such event does happen, the author apologizes in advance.**

How to read this book

- Understanding the coincidences and similarities requires a thorough grasp of the new DGR theory and familiarity with terms such as "NEPs," "PEPs," "Push bands," and "Pull bands" commonly used in the book.
- Unless one understands these terms, it is extremely difficult to make sense of the arguments made subsequently.

- So, the first step should indeed be to read and understand the theory. How the theory was derived or reached is described in "My Journey through the third book". Although this knowledge is not mandatory it is both interesting and helpful.
- Those in a hurry can skip it and just read the subsequent chapters explaining the theory in short and how is gravity explained, how is electromagnetic bonding explained.
- A section on Comparing DGR with General Relativity is given for better understanding although it may become too technical for some readers and one can skip it as well if one wishes to avoid too many technicalities.
- It is unavoidable to create a suitable background understanding of the theory of DGR and only then the real book starts.
- After understanding the basics of the theory, one can go to the contents and randomly choose what section to read.
- References to commonly held beliefs regarding deities are given in the form of Sanskrit Shlokas. They can provide interesting insights for those who understand Sanskrit. For those readers not understanding it, the English meanings of the verses are provided. The Sanskrit verses are given only as reference, knowing them or their meaning in detail is not mandatory to understand the contents of the book and some readers can ignore them.
- The theory is presented here in much less detail, and there are many aspects that cannot be fully discussed. Consequently, only the essential elements are shared. For

those interested in gaining a deeper understanding of the theory and to find answers to the following questions

1. how String theory emerges out of the theory,
2. how the theory explains Quantum Chromodynamics and phenomena occurring in the Nucleus,
3. how the theory explains MOND,
4. what is inertia and how DGR explains it etc

Are referred to my third book namely "Decoding Gravity Time and Causality" which is freely available throughout India on Amazon, Flipkart and publishers' websites at Notion press https://notionpress.com/en/ind/login.

https://notionpress.com/read/decoding-gravity-time-and-causality/hardcover

Alternatively, one can subscribe and see the videos at

https://www.youtube.com/@rohitkale6380

especially see the video

https://youtu.be/0vkXjcHSZLU?si=W4Szj8P9brKQGuPw

Why Physics needs a new Direction?

The trouble with today's Physics

Welcome to today's physics. Today, it has been more than a century since General Relativity (GR) and 60 years since Quantum mechanics (QM). There has been no significant advance in Fundamentals of Physics since then.

We have two theories of Physics that are considered highly successful and well-tested. GR however has trouble getting along with QM since they are fundamentally different. GR is classical and QM is not. GR assumes a married spacetime, has variable time with no Universal simultaneity and a space that is an active player. QM on the other hand has a fixed background entity of time with universal simultaneity, a fixed background entity of space not actively participating in any force exchange which is not married to time with many force-carrying particles that bring about the exchange of forces.

Reconciliating the two is currently impossible in their current forms. GR cannot explain the spacetime curvature needed to explain the most commonly performed experiment, "the falling apple".

GR is unable to explain many other experimental findings like "Flat rotation curves of Galaxy" and gravity provided by it falls significantly short of explaining Gravitational lensing of Galaxy clusters, for both of which one has to speculate the existence of a yet unknown entity called Dark matter. In essence, what is said is that what we know about the Universe is 5%. The remaining 95% constitutes Dark matter and Dark energy, both of which are unsolved mysteries.

QM has many troubling entities like superposition, entanglement, the spin of charged particles, and wave-particle duality of light and particles – all of which have good evidence but are ill-understood yet.

If you want to prove GR wrong, just do one experiment – the double-slit experiment. Its results cannot be explained whatsoever by GR.

If you want to prove QM wrong, just feed the Gravitational lensing data. And the theory crashes. QM and its weirdness cannot explain lensing.

Thus, both these theories are half-truths and everyone knows that there is a high likelihood of an underlying truth, a theory that reconciles the two. Such a theory is called ***the Theory of Quantum Gravity***. If it explains all the four fundamental forces of Nature, then it becomes ***a Theory of Everything.***

Not even Wrong

The only known attempt to reconcile the two theories is the String Theory. But Prof Peter Voit in his book

"Not Even Wrong" gives the myriad problems of String theory including its complete lack of falsifiability and ability to make predictions. The whole theory constitutes just beautiful Math. Although beautiful mathematically, the theory predicts a Multiverse and can encompass all possibilities with infinite changeability. There are 10^{500} different possibilities that need to be researched. And it needs 11 Dimensions. Even if all manpower in physics research focused on this for hundreds of years, we would still only scratch the surface.

There is no likelihood of anything to change in the future.

Lost in Math

Sabine Hossenfelder, a renowned author and physicist, discusses the challenges facing modern physics in her book of the same name. She argues that the field is in deep trouble due to a lack of direction. A significant factor contributing to this issue is the unwillingness of physicists to change their flawed methodologies, including an excessive obsession with "beauty."

The Funding Trap

The faulty system of Academia and Institutional hierarchies and selective funding has led to most Physics manpower working only on String Theory while other approaches get little funding. The Publish or perish obsession in academia means that the physicists working on alternative approaches to foundations of Physics don't get published and so don't get funding or prominent positions in reputed Physics departments.

The problems In Publication process

The peer review process is riddled with selection bias, author bias, stereotypical bias, confirmation bias, Editorial bias and many such biases so that authors with alternative viewpoints are unlikely to get through the peer review process in reputed journals.

The Obsession with endless Publications with no result – The Curse of Knowledge

The paper publication rate of physicists has increased tremendously. But the fruitful results coming out of their publications is reduced. Most publications don't get enough citations and self-citation has become the unwritten rule. Thousands of academic papers are being published but the real output of break-through publications has vanished. Most of these papers are so deep into theoretical realm that they are beyond comprehension even for distinguished physicists belonging to a slightly different specialty. The papers written with the layman in mind never get published citing the reason "not having enough scientific vigour"

The trouble with Academia and the system

Bias in the hiring process and funding process significantly limits the choices in which people can carry on research. Thus, only one or two approaches get more funding and the diversity of approaches is actively prevented. There is no guarantee that the approaches that get funding are the correct approaches to understand Quantum Gravity.

The Parroting

People engaged in theoretical discussions actively avoid contrary viewpoints making it extremely difficult for them to keep up to date with approaches other than the one they are engaged in. Thus, the Conferences and discussions are also completely divided into Stringy conferences focussed only on String Theory or Loopy conferences discussing only Loop Quantum Gravity.

The saying "You scratch my back – I will scratch yours" has become a reality.

The Confirmation bias in Physics

The teams engaged in huge machines like the Large Hadron Collider in CERN in Switzerland, have acknowledged that more than 99.99% of the data coming out from the collider is discarded as noise. Thus, we selectively use only the data that confirms our preconceptions while actively filtering the Data that rejects our beliefs.

(For reference check out:

1. https://profmattstrassler.com/articles-and-posts/largehadroncolliderfaq/the-trigger-discarding-all-but-the-gold/

2. https://atlas.cern/Updates/Briefing/Signal-Noise)

The "more energetic collider needed?" conundrum

Most theoretical predictions have gone beyond the testable range. There is an endless list of expensive experiments with heavy machines built for detecting specific theoretical predictions with negative results. Despite so many negative results, the ability to give up certain approaches and think beyond one's preconceptions is no longer a virtue. Current theories are designed to be infinitely modifiable and can explain any experimental result.

Rising number of conundrums

There are many unanswered questions including the possibility of accelerated expansion of the Universe, information loss paradox, vacuum catastrophe and the recent weird results by the James Webb telescope showing well-formed Galaxies in the Early Universe and some Galaxies older than the estimated age of the Universe.

Is there hope?

Isaac Newton once said

"If I have seen further, it is by standing on the shoulders of giants"

In my third book, I described a new approach to Quantum Gravity. An approach which admits that both QM and GR are partially wrong despite being partially right. The approach wasn't new and many people worked on it before as well. An approach where the Speed of light is not constant but variable. Einstein described it first in his paper. Many giants like Paul Dirac have also thought or contributed their bit in this direction while describing the "Sea of Electrons" theory and the Large Number Hypothesis. Mordehai Milgrom, while describing his theory of Modified Newtonian Dynamics, contributed in this direction. There were many things common between all these. The willingness to think out of the box. The readiness to think differently and the modesty to accept that some of their presumptions could be wrong. They failed not because they were less capable, but because they did not have all the pieces of the puzzle. One of their mistakes was excessive “zooming in” instead of “zooming out” that was needed. A theory of everything must incorporate all the known theories from all subjects. The zooming-in will eventually happen later.

Hope or waste of time?

The theory I refer to as "Dynamic General Relativity" (DGR) is akin to a distant relative of General Relativity. It is more accessible than many physics theories and can be explained in a way that even kindergarteners can understand. DGR relies on just a few key assumptions, which enable it to accomplish significant achievements.

It can

- Successfully reconcile QM and GR
- Explain variable time and curved space
- Explain energy
- Explain light, explain what is waving
- Explain inertia
- Explain all four fundamental forces of nature
- Explain what is electric flux/magnetic flux,
- Explain electromagnetic bonding and chemistry
- Explain the weird findings of the double-slit experiment
- Explain why we see superposition
- Explain the spin of a charged particle

- Explain the wave-particle duality of light and particles
- Explain Gravitational lensing, Gravitational redshift,
- Explains Galaxy rotation curves with MOND and avoids the need for Dark matter
- Explains Matter antimatter asymmetry
- Has the potential to make precise predictions and has the potential to be confirmed by experimental verification

(Just to name a few).

Detailed explanations of these cannot be included in this book as the purpose of this book is different. For those who are interested, everything is explained in my previous book "Decoding Gravity Time and Causality"

However, the theory is explained in short in this book as well to get a basic understanding of what DGR is and how it is different from other accepted theories.

The theory is just in its infancy and a lot needs to be done before it can be accepted as a scientific theory.

Disclaimers

Disclaimers

Before reading this book, one should be clear about certain things given below.

The Author

I am a doctor by profession and do not have a Physics background. You can call Physics my obsession.

I am an author and I have authored three books yet. The journey through writing them was extremely pleasurable and enlightening.

Professor Lee Smolin, the author of the book "The Trouble with Physics" once said

"Deep and persistent problems are never solved by accident. They are solved only by people who are obsessed with them and set out to solve them directly"

How Physics became an obsession is a long story and this isn't the right place to discuss it. But I believe that there is a reason for everything.

The reason, I believe, I reached my third book on Physics namely "Decoding Gravity, Time and Causality" and now this book, is because I understood Human Psychology. The reason I understood Human Psychology (at least to some extent) is because I got obsessed with the reasons behind Humans taking wrong decisions while writing my first book "How the Homo Sapiens Blundered" and this obsession with Human Psyche led to my second book "Decoding Human Psyche". Understanding the Psychology of Humans including Physicists enabled me to do what was needed to reach this theory – Lateral thinking i.e. Thinking beyond the firm preconceptions or beliefs of modern Physics.

In "Decoding Gravity Time and Causality" I have described a theory that can be called a "Theory of Quantum Gravity and a Theory of Everything". I called it Dynamic General Relativity, just to stress that it is a special form of General Relativity with a non-curved dynamically moving Spacetime and variability of the speed of light.

But while this theory took shape, I realised something deeper. I came across some extreme coincidences and I knew that at some point in time, I have to write my fourth book to document these coincidences.

The author is not a Ved Acharya.

I do not have a Vedantic background, nor am I a Vedic scholar. I haven't read any Puranic scriptures. The beliefs discussed in this book are commonly recognized by all Sanatani Hindus. I was able to find references for some of these beliefs in well-known Sanskrit shlokas or mantras, but for others, I do not have any references.

The author is not a Physics expert.

As discussed before, I am not a professional physicist, and I do not hold any professional degree in Physics. My professional degrees are in Medicine.

My journey through the Third book

My journey through the third book

In this section, I have briefly described the logical thinking behind the derivation of this new theory of Quantum Gravity called Dynamic General Relativity that I described in full detail in my third book (Decoding Gravity Time and Causality). This section may become too technical and boring for some readers as it is unrelated to the Trideva and is meant for better understanding of DGR. To me, it seems essential that one has some background knowledge of what DGR is and what logical thinking led to its development. But those in a hurry can skip this section and directly go to the section "DGR, the Theory of Everything - in short")

How I reached DGR

Since an early age, I have been fascinated by the falling apple in Newton's experiment, one that is repeated trillions of times daily worldwide using different objects. What pulls all of us towards the Earth and keeps us from flying off to space? A question I often asked myself. How can an invisible string keep pulling the ball down even after I throw it with so much force?

Newtonian gravity made sense. When I learned about the term forces, I acknowledged that there is some truth in it. Like Newton, I too pondered how gravity acted over vast distances without any medium in between. This "action at a distance" dilemma unsettled Newton.

As I studied basic physics in school and read about Newton's laws and the concept of inertia, I became curious about the origin of this intriguing force. Inertia keeps a moving body in motion and is what causes us to jolt forward against the dashboard when the driver suddenly hits the brakes. To my young and inexperienced mind, Newton's second law seemed counterintuitive. How could a body in motion continue moving without anything pushing it forward? Additionally, I was amazed by how few people questioned these concepts.

As I understood more complex physics, my confusion, far from being resolved, was further aggravated by the Special and General Relativity theories of Albert Einstein. How can the curvature of spacetime explain the Newtonian apple? I wondered.

Is GR Right or Wrong?

Although the "action at a distance conundrum" was partially resolved, Einstein's theories left their unique enigmas. What the hell is this variable time? How can clocks tick at different paces nearer the Earth's surface (Gravitational time dilation) or in an accelerated frame of reference (time dilation due to motion)? This was fortunately not the plight of me alone but of every kid or teenager trying to make sense of Physics. These confusing concepts kept tickling me in my imagination. I often discussed these topics with my elder brother Chetan. When he told me that if we keep going straight in one direction with a spaceship, after a long time we might end up in the same spot again. This is like moving along the Earth's surface, travelling all around the circumference of the Earth without ever realizing that we moved along a curved path.

He also told me about "Black Holes" and the fact that light can travel all around a massive black hole as the space-time around the black hole beyond the edge or event horizon is curved and is almost like a circle. Although I initially did not believe any of these to be true, after I came across Gravitational lensing, I stopped fighting with these difficult ideas.

Although I accepted them as right, I knew that there must be an underlying truth that most physicists are neglecting.

How can a theory that allows us to send large satellites into orbit or land robots on the moon (Newtonian Mechanics) be incorrect when we go closer to the sun?

The theory of General Relativity could successfully explain the "orbit of mercury problem". In short, the orbit of the planet Mercury showed precession or deviation which could not be explained by Newtonian gravity. However, GR explained it based on the curvature of the spacetime as it passes near the Sun.

There were many other confirmations and successes of the theory of GR. Sir Eddington successfully showed gravitational lensing due to the Sun's mass during the total Solar Eclipse. Another success was the demonstration of Gravitational time dilation and Time dilation due to motion. Accurate atomic clocks were used in multiple experiments to suggest that time runs slower nearer the surface of the Earth.

GPS and Gravitational time dilation

With the advent of GPS technology, accurately localizing objects using radio waves requires scientists to consider the curvature of spacetime and gravitational time dilation. Failing to account for these factors would lead to significant errors in location measurements. Therefore, every time someone uses a GPS system, they are essentially confirming the validity of general relativity.

Gravitational lensing has also been demonstrated so often now, that there is little doubt that GR is right. Even the demonstration that Gravitational waves exist and propagate with the speed of light proved GR right. The demonstration of a Black hole by the Event Horizon Telescope was another feather in the cap of successfully proven predictions of GR.

Doubts and holes in GR

Einstein published his paper on Special Relativity in 1905 and on General Relativity in 1915. He did not gain fame for his theory of GR until 1919 when Sir Eddington demonstrated the curvature of Spacetime due to the mass of the Sun. Einstein had already become sceptical about GR, much before Einstein became famous for his theory and it was universally accepted. His landmark paper on "Variable speed of light type of GR" published in 1911 showed that he suggested that a different slightly confusing version of GR is possible wherein the speed of light isn't constant but is variable in a straight "spacetime Universe" instead of the constant speed of light in a curved

Spacetime Universe and this variability of the speed of light is the reason for Gravitational lensing. This less-known paper did not get enough fame and thus is hardly known.

As I continued reading, I encountered several instances where scale plays a significant role. Even General Relativity, the most widely accepted theory of gravity, fails to account for phenomena at the scale of galaxies or intergalactic clusters. To explain the observed results, we either need to modify the laws of gravity (as proposed in MOND) or introduce additional, yet-to-be-discovered masses known as dark matter.

I had many doubts about General relativity and its complete inability to logically explain the falling apple despite being the most commonly performed experiment. I was further astonished when I found that Einstein had published the 1911 paper describing the "variable speed of light" type of General relativity as a possible alternative form of GR which was never accepted or given any importance. So, Einstein himself, at least at some point in his life did believe that his GR may be wrong or incompletely understood. Although his VSL type of GR did not receive much attention, I don't know the reason why he dropped the idea completely in his subsequent life. Or did he?

The GHG emissions bias in Climate science

While writing my second book, ***Decoding Human Psyche***, I had the opportunity to explore in detail how the human mind functions, and how humans—delusional creatures by nature—develop deeply ingrained belief systems that are incredibly difficult to break.

In writing my first book, ***How the Homo Sapiens Blundered,*** I came to understand that the issue of climate change has largely been hijacked by left-leaning political groups with a communist ideology. I realized that the climate lobby—including many highly intellectual climate scientists—focuses exclusively on the belief that "greenhouse gas emissions" are the primary cause of rising CO2 levels. In doing so, they overlook other critical crises facing humanity, such as the extinction crisis and the "insect apocalypse." Their solutions and recommendations are almost entirely centred around reducing GHG emissions, decarbonization, and bankrupting the petroleum industry.

With ***Decoding Human Psyche***, I began to understand how "anchoring beliefs" take root in the mind and how cycles of confirmation—focusing only on events that support a given belief—serve to strengthen that belief over time. Once a belief or preconception is established, the self-serving bias within the mind actively resists any attempt to challenge it or replace it with an alternative. To question one's own beliefs is to admit the possibility of being wrong, which requires a level of humility and emotional intelligence that is often lacking in left-leaning liberals. As a result, criticizing their recommendations—such as the promotion of wooden skyscrapers (which exacerbates deforestation and the biodiversity crisis), biofuels (which increase the demand for agricultural land), or policies that involve culling cows (because their methane emissions are considered harmful)—is often met with accusations of being a "climate denier" or even a moral transgression. Any attempt to consider alternative solutions is dismissed with rage.

The combination of congruence bias, confirmation bias, and self-serving bias can make it nearly impossible for individuals to think beyond their preconceptions.

Thinking beyond one's preconceptions is known as lateral thinking, or "thinking outside the box."

With a thorough understanding of these biases, I realized that human psychology is universally applicable. The same cognitive mechanisms that shape beliefs about climate change apply equally to the mind of a physicist, for example.

Even a physicist might resist ideas that challenge their ego or their preconceived notions. These beliefs can be very hard to break. Einstein himself broke many of the prevailing beliefs in physics during his time, including concepts such as mass-energy equivalence, the variability of time, and the idea of light as a particle (the photon), to name a few.

The fame that Einstein garnered from Eddington's confirmation of the bending of light by the gravity of the Sun during the 1919 solar eclipse experiment had a profound impact on physicists of that era. The overwhelming success of general relativity, supported by subsequent confirmations such as gravitational lensing and redshift, likely reinforced the bias among physicists, making it difficult for them to entertain similar-looking, but "uglier," alternative theories. The powerful bias created by Einstein's groundbreaking theory may have contributed to a reluctance to consider its potential flaws.

Psychology helps

I was aware of the functioning of the mind and the biases and their blocking effect, preventing experts from thinking beyond their prejudices.

I was, however, also very well aware of the Dunning Kruger effect and its possible effects on my mind while I tried to prove the entire Climate science community and the entire Fundamentals of Physics community wrong or biased. This bias or tendency of the mind makes us overestimate our abilities and introduce a belief that I am always right or that others opposing my views are always wrong.

I constantly scrutinized myself for an exaggerated sense of knowledge. Fortunately, my extreme distance from anything close to being a physicist helped keep all these unwanted beliefs away and it gave me an extraordinary freedom to think in any lines I needed to crack the conundrum of Gravity.

Friction between General Relativity and Quantum mechanics

With further reading, I came across the friction between GR and Quantum mechanics.

I have come to understand that some experts in physics are asserting that there is a crisis in the field. After the developments of General Relativity (GR) and Quantum Mechanics, they believe there has been no significant advancement in our understanding of physics. Despite the billions of dollars invested in constructing large-scale facilities like particle accelerators and dark matter detectors, these efforts have yielded few results.

I came across various attempts to fill in the gaps in the fundamentals of physics with Loop Quantum Gravity and String Theory. Although I lacked an understanding of the complex mathematics involved, I could see that both of them have the problem of tunnel vision and have a good chance of being partially right. I could almost read the minds of these physicists within their eco chambers, attending their Loopy or Stringy conferences and getting agitated or not understanding the papers on the topic outside their field of interest. I saw them falling deep into their metaphorical rabbit holes and more importantly, I saw no attempt on their parts to come out. The loopy physicists were busy proving that time doesn't exist while stringy physicists are busy finding extra dimensions and also working out the math of the 10^{500} different potential manifolds their theory predicts.

Loop Quantum Gravity (LQG)

I was pretty fascinated by LQG and the Planck units which formed a part of its basic assumptions. Only later did I realise that LQG was beautiful only from a distance. As one went deep into its mathematics, it would steer into the disappearance of time. Although it has not succeeded yet, it still is one of the theories of Quantum Gravity that has the potential to be proven right (or wrong) i.e. is testable in principle. The reason I was attracted to it was its potential to contribute to phenomenology. The idea that we "Shut up and calculate" but don't ask what exactly is happening within the orbits of atoms or between charged particles like Electrons or Protons or Quarks within the nucleus was obnoxious to my mind.

So, I started imagining what it would be like at Planck scale. I was pretty fascinated by the idea that there can be an indivisible atom equivalent of space called a Planck compartment. I started imagining the Newtonian apple falling down and at the moment it is in a free fall, the space beneath it up to the surface of the Earth divided into multiple cubical regions with known volume or better with 1 Planck volume. As time moves forward, the distance between the apple and the Earth reduces, and so does the number of these cubicle spaces. If we imagine a stack of these Planck compartments arranged underneath the apple, the stack keeps reducing as the apple approaches the Earth's surface due to Gravity. It made sense that the number would keep reducing. "Where are these PCs going?" I wondered.

Quantum foam and the birth of a new Theory

Soon enough, I realised that they were being destroyed.

As I read Quantum mechanics, I read that in these miniature realms, spontaneously appearing or disappearing particles aren't that implausible.

When I read about the "Quantum foam" with particles and antiparticles being formed spontaneously and annihilating spontaneously at Planck scales, I saw a possible solution.

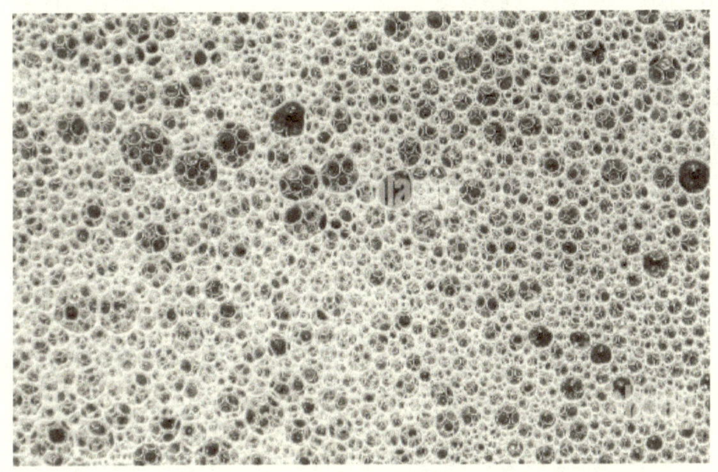

Figure: Quantum Foam

What is the rate of formation of these pairs per unit time?

Can this rate be the same everywhere?

or

Can it vary from place to place?

It was clear that a person knowing Special Relativity wouldn't ask such a question as for them, there is no universally applicable background entity of time. So, this time interval varies at every point for them. Or is it that the variable time of Special Relativity is the reason why a relatively constant rate seems variable to us? Physicists compulsively think of a fixed background time while thinking of QM and a variable time while thinking of the larger phenomena in the realm of GR.

However, I had no such compulsions in my mind, my mind being free from such biases. In the current physicist's mind, completely different rules for a miniature Quantum particle and completely different rules for the larger realms did not create any conflict. However, in my mind, I knew that the fact that there is continuity I.e. there is a single universe, it cannot have two different sets of rules. The rules have to be something in between the two extremes.

My mind wasn't satisfied by two different theories, one for the small and the other for the big. It needed a single set of rules.

Can this process of "particle and antiparticle pairs forming and annihilating contribute to volume?

If you ask a person expert in Quantum mechanics, he would say they aren't real, but virtual, they don't contribute to volume. It is all just Math. But fortunately, I wasn't an expert in Quantum mechanics and so I had no such compulsions.

My mind was free to wander wherever needed. There was however a risk of getting lost. But physics is already getting lost in higher dimensions, unreal time and multiverse. So, what can be the worst-case scenario? It would definitely not be worse than hundreds of thousands of papers on fundamental physics and quantum gravity taking physics nowhere, I thought.

So, I persisted.

Early triumphs: Actively Expanding or Contracting space

What if there is a universal background time? What if these pairs do contribute to volume? And what if there is a definable rate of appearance and disappearance? What if this rate varies from place to place?

If these pairs are created faster and the annihilation lags behind at one point in space, more Particle-Antiparticle pairs would be created and fewer would be destroyed. More volume would mean expanding space.

Opposed to that, if the process of destruction dominates, active loss of volume, i.e. actively contracting space.

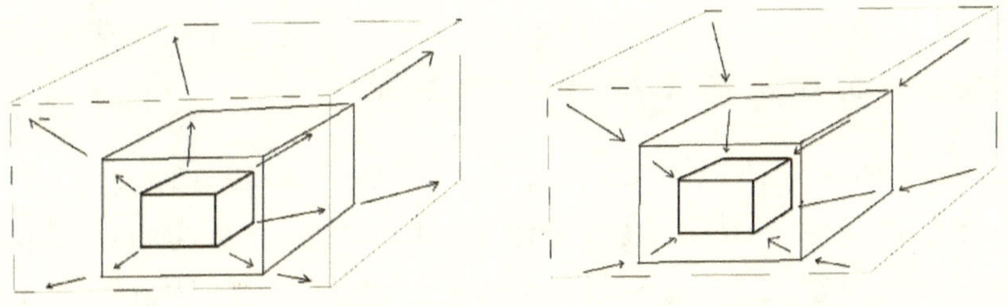

Figure: Shows an actively expanding space on the left and an actively contracting space on the right

I knew that multiple events of such expanding space at Planck levels could easily add up to give rise to a bigger volume of expansion. I also somehow felt that given the size of the Universe, there should not be any upper limit to the number of events.

I learned that the Universe is expanding after the Hubble telescope observed the redshift of distant stars. This can explain both the expanding Universe and also the actively contracting space under the Newtonian apple.

This early triumph sparked my excitement, and I continued my reading. Soon, I encountered Eric Verlinde's theory known as "Entropic Gravity." I realized that the idea of varying entropy as a cause of gravity is not new and has been explored in the past.

(In Entropic Gravity as described by Eric for non-physicists to understand, Gravity is an ultimate consequence of multiple events. He gave an example of a long protein molecule responsible for elasticity. Small changes in the shape or configuration of the linear molecule at multiple locations along its length, keep adding up to reduce the length of the molecule or pull the two ends together.)

Because I knew the concept of tunnel vision and knew that I was not aware of most of the attempts to describe Gravity, I kind of expected this. And reading a bit of Eric's theory added to my excitement rather than depressing me that someone attempted and couldn't succeed. I had nothing to lose if the attempts failed. So, there was no fear of a defeat.

Newtonian falling apple and Einsteinian curved space time

I started imagining cubes under the Newtonian apple with 1 cm sides. As the apple falls, the upper cubes lose volume slower while the lower ones lose volume faster, and the cubes get distorted.

What would happen when they reach the surface?

And what are these Cubes surrounded by?

The answer to the second question was pretty clear. They are surrounded by more such cubes that are made of Planck compartments stacked together.

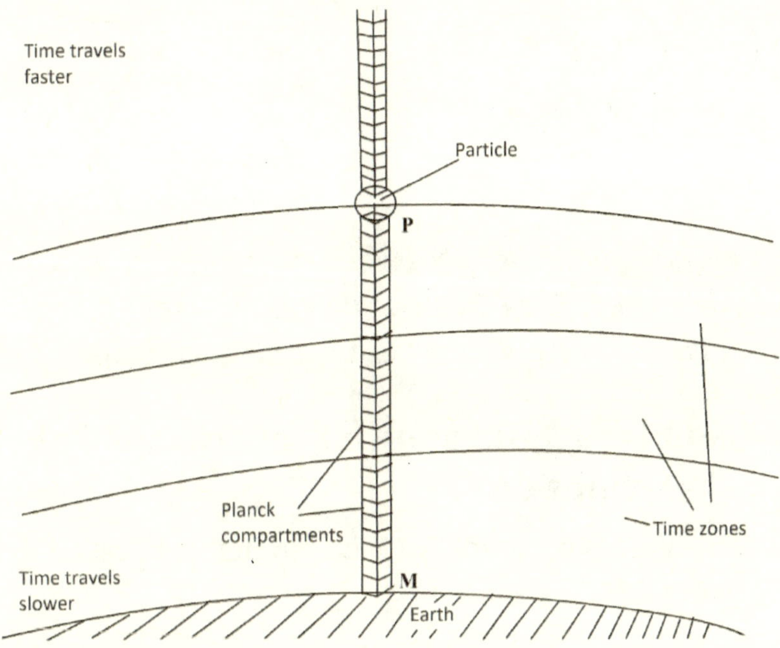

Figure: Shows a particle P suspended in Gravitational time dilation zones of the Earth. A skyscraper of compartments 1mm^3*, 1cm*^{3} *or 1m*^{3} *extending from point P to point M on the Earth's surface is shown. Each of these compartments will lie in different time zones and as per DGR will lose volume actively and contract, thus pulling the particle P downwards.*

But as the cubes contract or expand, what happens to the surrounding space? If there is no Compensatory contraction or expansion, we would see a void. We don't see one? So, the fabric of space-time must have some elasticity. There must be some energy within the space-time that prevents void formation.

An additional assumption was introduced in the theory to provide elasticity to spacetime.

Figure: Shows what happens when the central PC vanishes or is destroyed. The PC void or PC vacuum created is not allowed and pulls the PCs towards each other.

The "No PC vacuum allowed" or "No Void allowed" assumption

Between two PCs, there will be something called true nothingness or PC vacuum.

But this PC vacuum would not let the PCs remain separate and would pull them together. But if there is active destruction of PCs at a point, a void will be created. This void will pull the PCs at the edge towards the centre. That is, a void would lead to active contraction of the surrounding spherical region of space. The spherical region immediately adjacent to that would follow. This will form a wave of contracting space. This wave would keep moving outwards with every destruction event. If there are ten destruction events, for example, there will be ten waves moving outwards.

This should work even for creation. At a point of excessive creation, the surrounding spherical regions would be pushed apart, creating a void that necessitates further creation to compensate for the void.

The theory thus predicted that at every particle with positive mass there would be active destruction of PCs happening with actively contracting space around it. At every particle with negative mass i.e. having negative energy, there would be active creation happening with an actively expanding space around it. This compensatory active spatial contraction and expansion can curve the space and bend the path of a passing photon successfully explaining Einsteinian curved space.

I knew Einstein's theories in principle although I wasn't aware of the complex mathematics involved.

I knew $E=mc^2$

I.e. energy correlates with mass or rather they are the same or they are interconvertible.

I knew that a huge amount of energy resides within the Nucleus given the might of the atomic bomb that exploded in Hiroshima and given that this energy can be extracted in nuclear reactors.

Soon I realised that the particles might have positive energy and antiparticles have negative energy. I came across the famous physicist Paul Dirac and his excellent work on antimatter (as suggested by one of my close friends Abhishek Ganguly.)

I read a lot about Quantum mechanics and its weirdness with particles disappearing and reappearing, being in a superposition of multiple states at once and being a particle and wave at the same time. I read about the friction between GR and QM. I also read about the various failed attempts to make sense of GR and QM put together.

What is right, QM or GR?

For me, a good theory is one that has minimum assumptions. More are the assumptions needed; more is the likelihood that one assumption may be wrong.

A theory with infinite assumptions would be a bad theory. This is why I was repelled by the thought of a Multiverse or Everett's "Many-worlds interpretation" of QM.

I understand that it is easier to disprove a scientific theory than to prove it. You only need one experimental result that contradicts the predictions of a theory. There have been several widely accepted theories that have made predictions inconsistent with experimental observations.

One such example is GR. It could not predict any of the observations of QM. GR is a classical theory and needs a particle to have a fixed well-defined coordinate in space. If the particle is at multiple locations at once, out of the many locations, where will the curvature of space-time be due to the presence of a mass equivalent to high energy within it? GR has been proven millions of times by gravitational lensing experiments and by atomic clocks that measure the time dilation due to gravity. That said, if we do a single experiment of "double slit experiment," its findings cannot be explained by GR and one has to take help from QM.

Similarly, a single Gravitational lensing or time dilation experiment proves QM wrong. These indicated that both of them could be partially correct and partially wrong. Some physicists believe in these two theories so well that they believe we live in a dual type of universe where the rules differ with scale. Some, however, do acknowledge that there is probably a common underlying theory called the Theory of Everything that explains both.

The Photon Clock and the variable time

I had heard of the photon clock and Einstein's thought experiments. They fascinated me. I started imagining a photon bouncing in between two mirrors. If space actively contracts behind it, it would reach the edge mirrors slowly. If the space actively expands, it will reach faster. Would that lead to a slower or faster ticking of the photon clock? If the most sensitive photon clock can't differentiate this effect of active expansion or contraction of space on the measured time, can our routine atomic clocks detect it/differentiate it/measure it? The emergence of a variable time in our actively expanding or contracting space meant that Dynamic General Relativity did explain GR and its predictions. I soon realised that if multiple regions around the Earth at a distance from the surface are contracting, they would form an inward-moving spherical region of space.

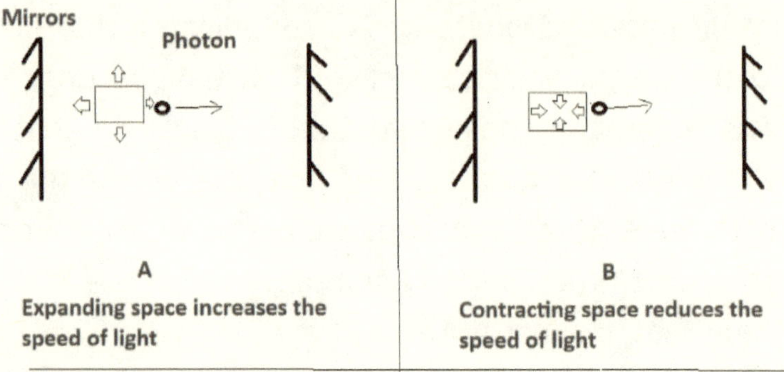

Arriving at the Basics of Dynamic General Relativity

Now I started imagining Planck-length-sized spheres all around the Earth falling inwards. (see EPCAs in the section explaining the theory in short)

Soon I realised that once a sphere moves in, something has to pull the outer sphere. Just like a vacuum is created between the two. I called it a Planck vacuum as it is not a true vacuum. It became clear that space should not only be made up of small atoms of space but also have elasticity. This is possible only with a "no PC vacuum allowed" assumption.

What I needed were three processes. Active destruction of Planck compartments, active creation of PCs and some mechanism to maintain balance by giving elasticity to the fabric of space.

The first glimpse of "the Trideva"

This is the point where I came across the first glimpse of "the Trideva".

The Vedic texts propounded that this universe (Srishti) has three Gunas I.e. Trigunatmak i.e. has three characteristics.

I knew that for the spheres to fall towards the Earth, destruction has to happen incessantly at the centre.

Constant destruction at the centre and sustenance leading to spheres of PCs falling inwards was a pretty good logical way of explaining the falling apple.

I imagined a rubber duck toy floating on the water in a tub. As soon as you remove the stopper and water starts flowing out of the tub, the level of water keeps dropping and the distance between the floor and the duck reduces. This thought fascinated me. The PCs are literally being flushed out of this Universe. But where? Where are they going? To another realm? Another Universe? So, is there a wormhole for Planck compartments at the centre of every particle with mass?

These ideas are not new. It is well known that GR supports the existence of black holes and wormholes.

"What is the speed with which these PC spheres would fall?" I thought.

And based on what time?

Also, how many events of destruction would be needed at the centre to match the gravitational attraction of the Earth? (These questions are unfortunately still unanswered yet and need derivation of math of DGR which is quite a task and would need supercomputers to derive.)

Contradictions with SR and GR?

If GR or SR is to be believed, there is no universally equal time and there is no universal spontaneity.

Here I found the need to have a universal time, something Einstein called T_0 indicating the time of an observer at an infinite distance from the Gravitating object.

Although here the theory was starting to contradict Special Relativity, I was fearless.

I noted that there are already some theories proposing a variable velocity of light as an alternative to the theory of Inflationary cosmology. So, I felt confident. Although my approach was completely different, the theory that came out wasn't very different from what was already described.

How does it have a variable speed of light and still doesn't violate SR?

In DGR, the actively expanding space behind a photon make it move forwards faster thus increasing the value of c. In case, there is actively contracting space behind the photon, its forward propagation is hampered and it slows down i.e. value of c reduces. The value of c completely depends on status of contraction or expansion of the surrounding space. However, this variability is only with respect to Universal time. With increase in value of c, local time gets contracted. While with decrease in value of c, local time gets dilated. Thus, with respect to the Local time, c remains constant and variability of the velocity of the photon is only measured with respect to Universal time. Thus, it doesn't violate SR but it actually provides an explanation for the apparent constancy of c. In GR, constancy of c has to be added as an assumption while in DGR, it emerges effortlessly.

There were however significant hurdles. Newton believed that Gravity travels instantaneously at an almost infinite speed. Einstein's theories suggested that it travels at the speed of light as the speed of light is the upper limit to causality. However, the theory conflicts itself when it further says that there is no limit to how fast space can expand or contract and edges of the observable Universe may be receding from us faster than the speed of light and we will never be able to see them. Looking at Dynamic General Relativity's perspective, the expansion or contraction of space would be the movement of the Planck compartments.

The size of "the Present"

If a PC moves with the development of the PC vacuum with each inward movement of the PC spherical aggregate, how fast can the PC react? This led me to the conundrum of "How small is the Present?" Is Planck time the lowest possible time? Can a PC react only after 1 Planck time has passed? A Planck time is extremely tiny, about 10^{-43}sec. Although it is unfathomably small for humans, it is nothing for nature. Of course, if there is a lower limit to space in Dynamic General Relativity, is there a lower limit to time as well?

If there is a lower limit to it, that is smaller time intervals don't exist, it leads to many restrictions. If Planck time is the smallest, the Einsteinian speed limit would hold. This means that causality will have a speed limit and it would make sense that light or other EM waves pass with the speed of light. But this would set a limit to the reaction time of the neighbouring Planck compartments and thus the space would have significant restrictions on how fast it can move. Thus, although I kept this possibility at the back of my mind, I decided to let it go and assumed that smaller time intervals should be allowable, that is the smallest time interval possible is significantly smaller than 1 Planck time. This meant that "faster than speed-of-light" passage of information would become possible with an actively contracting space and a reacting neighbouring region of space. This saved the inside of a Black hole within the event horizon with space moving inwards faster than the speed of light- I thought. This however had significant contradictions to GR, as it meant that Gravity would travel significantly faster than the speed of light. This matched with the Newtonian view somewhat, which is that Gravity travelled almost instantaneously. But it contradicted the recent detection of Gravitational waves that came along with cosmic radiation suggesting that Gravitational waves travelled with the speed of light. Indeed, the Gravitational waves detected may be slightly different than the Time resetting waves that lead to Gravitational pull. This became clearer after I was thinking about Inertia and the propagation of a photon vs the propagation of a particle. The inward movement of the space within a particle-with-mass would happen much faster than the speed of light while within a photon, the energy locked in is much less and thus the inwards movement is expected to be lesser. The particle-with-mass, thus, has a limit for forward propagation. A detailed explanation of this is not possible here in this book. However, as is explained in subsequent sections, Push bands and Pull bands form faster than the speed of light in the longitudinal direction but drift outwards with the speed of light. Similarly, the Gravitational time resetting waves move faster than the speed of light but the drifting of disturbance caused by merging black holes may be drifting outward with the speed of light.

Paul Dirac and negative energy

I came across the work of Dirac and realised that he had suggested a similar theory with Electrons and Electron holes to explain the "Negative energies" that a particle could have. The concept of a "negative energy" in a particle was considerably resisted at the start but was welcomed without a doubt with the eventual detection of an "Antimatter" particle. However, nobody knew how these antimatter particles form and why they seem to be so rare and unstable. Logically it made sense that matter and antimatter particles would form together and can annihilate together as well. Why do we see only matter particles or positive energy particles? Where did all the corresponding antimatter particles go? This "Matter-Antimatter asymmetry" is still an unsolved mystery.

Another marvellous out-of-the-box idea from Paul Dirac was the Large Number Hypothesis. In this, Dirac found the absolute co-incidence that the total number of particles in the Universe is directly proportional to the age of the Universe suggesting that there should be places in the Universe where Hadrons are actively being created (Note that Hadrons are particles like electrons/protons etc that are accelerated and their collisions are studied in the Large Hadron Collider).

There were many ugly implications of this and thus nobody took it seriously.

What is the origin of G?

This idea is somewhat based on Mach's principle. In this, the gravitational constant G is related directly to the mass of the Universe and is variable.

I knew that the gravitational constant G is an extremely small number and thus it causes a significant reduction in the Gravitational pull between the two Gravitationally interacting bodies. If G was not there, the Gravitational attraction would be stronger.

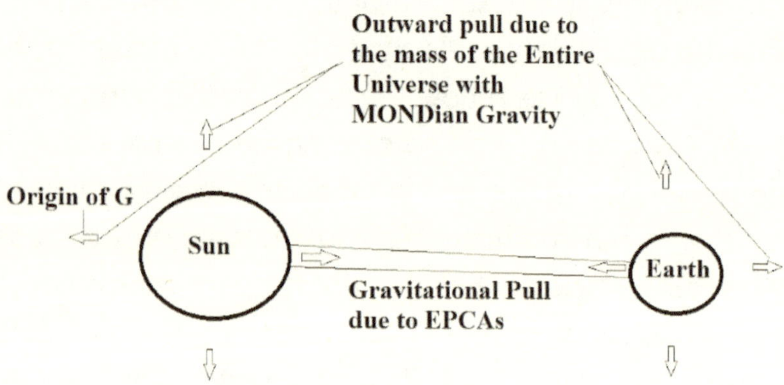

Figure: shows the probable origin of G which reduces the overall Gravitational pull of the Gravitating objects like the Sun and the Earth. This could possibly be due to the mass of the entire rest of the Universe exerting a MONDian force on the two objects effectively opposing their Gravitation.

It is as if some force is pulling the two gravitating bodies apart. Mach's principle says that the effect of mass distribution of the rest of the Universe, somehow, instantaneously travels from its diverse locations around the bodies and pulls the bodies apart. This outward pull isn't good enough to completely nullify the Gravity yet.

These weird-looking but exciting ideas matched perfectly with Dynamic General Relativity and excited me much more than the weird "Everett's Many-Worlds interpretation" like ideas wherein every moment breaks down into infinite universes.

When I came across "Loop Quantum Gravity" and was in the process of literally stealing some assumptions from it, I came across some attempts to derive its predictions and prove them right. One of the predictions is "massive" photons. If higher energy photons have mass, they would move slightly slower. This means that the higher energy radiation emitted from an event like a Supernova (which gives out radiation over the entire EM spectrum) would reach the Earth slower than the smaller frequency radiation. This was however not seen. Although the experiment had failed, it showed me a way. I heard quite a few times that a hadron or any particle for that matter gets mass because of the so-called "God particle" or the Higgs boson described first by Peter Higgs and detected in the Large Hadron Collider recently. The Higgs mechanism, as explained to all the lay people by physicists, is that there exists a field called the Higgs field present everywhere in this Universe. Particles with excessive mass interact with this field more and particles with no mass don't interact at all. This was pretty similar to what I was imagining as a particle.

The Photon

I imagined the destruction of space happening at a single PC and its compensation with an inward movement of a PC sphere reacting faster than a Planck time. This reactionary inward movement creates another PC vacuum around it causing another reactionary inward movement of the outer PC sphere. These inward-moving spheres would create a reactionary wave moving outwards. There should not be any inhibition to the number of destruction events that can happen at a single point, I hoped. I called these waves time-resetting waves. I realized that the more the events per Planck time, the faster the reactionary inward movement and to a greater distance per Planck time the reactionary wave would progress in a Planck time. I realized that this seemed similar to the Higgs mechanism. However, here there is no Higgs's boson. Or one can say that these spherical time-resetting waves could be equivalent to Higgs's boson.

I had a realization that a single event of destruction per Planck time would mean that the photon at the miniature Photon clock at this Planck compartment would stop ticking i.e. time would be zero. Thus, I called it the T=0 compartment. I also knew that multiple T=0 compartments can stay at a single compartment with multiple destruction events happening per Planck time. Space at the surrounding infalling "PC aggregates" which I called "EPCAs or eddy Planck compartment aggregates" would be in a state of contraction. The Photon clock placed here would show a dilated time. This time dilation would keep reducing as we go away from the centre.

The theory offered me a powerful way of imagining the events happening in the Planck realm. I realized that the T=0 compartment was like a "quantum" or "packet" of energy. Even the slightly dilated time in the EPCAs can be considered as energy. So, a Photon with higher energies would have a higher destruction happening at its core per Planck time and lower energy photons would have lesser destruction per Planck time happening within them.

By this, we can imagine the entire electromagnetic spectrum. The Theory however does predict these photons having some interaction with the surrounding space which is akin to the Higgs's field in Dynamic General Relativity. Does it mean that these photons have mass?

The triumph here was that I was able to explain the wave-particle duality of light with Dynamic General Relativity.

Wave particle duality of light

Newton considered light to be made up of particles. Huygen proposed that light is a wave. Following multiple experiments including those demonstrating reflection, refraction and especially interference patterns shown in a double slit experiment, it became clear that light is definitely a wave. What exactly is waving here was not known. However, the demonstration of the photoelectric effect and the proof that energy within light is directly proportional to the frequency and not intensity baffled everyone. Simply because this led to the Ultraviolet catastrophe. Mathematically, it meant that the energy in a wave would tend to infinity as frequency rises which meant that a body could lose infinite energy in a short period which was absurd. The description of a "Quantum" or a packet of light by Max Planck and then later the description of a photon by Einstein cleared the way for the existence of particles of light with different amounts of energy. Thus, light is now considered a wave as well as a particle.

"How is this possible or what does it even mean?

Nobody could answer this question satisfactorily before DGR. But with DGR, it becomes unambiguous. Photons are nothing but some PEPs aggregated together and thus have destruction happening within, with compensatory changes surrounding them. The destruction is not significant unlike a particle-with-mass and the inward movement of space around a Photon is not faster than light speed to a significant extent. Two photons would be separated by space with a mildly dilated time and space in active contraction. This is the DGR equivalent of entangled photons. As the energy of the photon increases, the extent of destruction per Planck time also rises.

Inertia at rest

With the particle of light and the wave in between decoded, I imagined the Space to be made of a thick magical jelly with a fish trapped within. The fish eats up the jelly but the magical jelly fills up the space quickly by repositioning the neighbouring particles of jelly. This "fish trapped in thick jelly" analogue can explain inertia at rest well.

Inertia in motion and kinetic energy

The particle in motion, however, needed much more than this simple analogy since the fish of "particle" in Dynamic General Relativity needed to eat up space from all sides equally. This was true for a static particle. What about a moving particle then? I thought...

Soon I realised that there will be two distinct directions for a moving particle, the preceding direction or towards the direction of motion of the particle and the receding one i.e. towards the direction opposite to the direction of motion of the particle. Our fish would eat up the jelly in both these directions equally when the particle is static but with unequal vigour when moving. Simply said, the particle eats up the Space faster towards the preceding border and the inward movement of EPCAs would be faster here. The eating up would be slower in the receding border and EPCAs would move inwards slower here. The difference between the two borders would represent the kinetic energy and is responsible for the inertia-in-motion.

A particle moving at high speeds would create a fresh uncompensated PC Vacuum in the receding border explaining the increase in mass due to velocity.

Another possible contributor to both inertia-at-rest and inertia-in-motion could be the MONDian gravity of the mass of the entire Universe although more work is needed in this regard.

The Double slit experiment (DSE)

It is impossible to explain all the various aspects of the Double slit experiment. But when a light wave reaches the two slits, two waves are produced which interfere with each other and produce an interference pattern. This interference pattern happens even if the light is thrown at the double slit, one photon at a time. The real weirdness starts when someone or some process is observing this Single photon DSE. The interference pattern disappears when there is a conscious observer or a camera observing the process.

What if, instead of a single photon, we throw electrons at the slits one at a time. A more intuitive result would be that the Electrons pass through one of the two slits (like a tennis ball) and eventually produce two bands corresponding to the two slits with no interference pattern. However, even the single electron DSE shows an interference pattern when there is no conscious observer and the pattern vanishes when an observer is present. Here, even single Electrons behave like waves, pass through both the slits, interfere with oneself and produce an interference pattern instead of the expected two bands.

These weird findings cannot be explained if we consider the electron as a classical spherical object. One has to take into account Quantum Mechanics. General Relativity invariably fails to explain the results. The Delayed choice Quantum Eraser type of DSE produces even weirder results and some authors have suggested "retro causality" i.e. transfer of information from future to past in explaining the findings. (details cannot be included here).

Unlike General Relativity, Dynamic General Relativity can very easily explain these results. In DGR, the photon has a variable amount of destruction within and waves associated with it all around. This means that DGR can explain the findings of DSE without the need for "superposition" wherein the quantum particle (here photon) is at multiple places at the same time i.e. passing through both the slits at the same time.

Even Electrons have waves associated with them to compensate for the destruction taking place within the particle.

Wave associated with the particle

When the Double slit experiment was performed with electrons instead of light, the results were interesting. When DSE was done with one electron at a time, it was expected that like a tennis ball does, the electron would pass through one of the two slits. If this was true, the electrons would eventually form two vertical strips. However, this did not happen. Even if electrons were passed one at a time, they eventually ended up in places on the screen akin to an interference pattern. This was true only if there were no conscious observers observing the photon. In the presence of a camera or observer, the interference pattern disappears and one gets two vertical stripes instead of the interference pattern.

This meant that the electron, instead of the expected behaviour of passing through one of the two slits, was able to pass through both slits at the same time and interfere with each other and form an interference pattern. There are many interpretations for this. The most accepted one is the Copenhagen interpretation wherein there occurs a collapse of the wave function, i.e. the electron is a wave (alternatively – the electron is a wave and particle at the same time – wave-particle duality) before and the wavefront collapses into a particle at the end. In DGR, the explanation is straightforward. The electron has a specific location at every point in time like what is advised by GR. The compensatory changes in the surrounding space happening due to the core and the lattice and also the spin and pole shifting leads to reverberatory movement of surrounding space that can be considered as the wave associated with the electron.

The wavefront of this wave can pass through both the slits, interferes with the wavefront entering from the other slit and the resultant interference pattern determines the position where the electron lands on the screen. This interpretation is equivalent to the Bohemian mechanics or Pilot wave interpretation of Quantum mechanics. Although, this does not explain why the interference no longer occurs in the presence of a conscious observer.

More work is needed in this regard.

MOND

Both Newtonian Gravity and General Relativity propose that the Gravitational field fades away proportional to the square of distance. The farther you go away from the body, the smaller the Gravitational pull. It was soon clear that this relation holds well up to our Solar system. Distances beyond that showed some anomalies. When scientists measured the velocities of stars at extreme distances from the Galactic centre at the periphery of the Galaxy, their velocities, instead of the expected progressive dip, showed a progressive rise which eventually flattened out and after a particular distance, the velocities of peripheral stars showed constant velocity.

Within the solar system, the gravitational pull due to the mass of the Sun keeps reducing as we move outwards and thus the force it can successfully counter would also reduce. It is interesting to imagine what would happen if the peripheral planets like Jupiter, Saturn, Uranus and Neptune behaved anomalously and had very high velocities. The centrifugal force due to circular motion would be too great and the inward-directed centripetal force of the Sun's gravity would prove to be insufficient and these planets would be thrown outwards long before life emerged on Earth.

Why is such a thing not happening to the outer stars in the Galaxies?

The Newtonian Gravity of the SMBH (Supermassive Black Hole) at the Galactic centre is not enough to hold these peripheral stars at the extremely high velocities shown by the data. These stars are so far away from the Galactic centre, possibly thousands of light years away, that they should have been thrown outwards immediately after forming i.e. would never form a part of the Galaxy.

This indicated that the Galaxy was behaving like a single large rotating disc and the relative position of the peripheral stars showed as if they were all bonded together and moving with the same velocity irrespective of the distance from the centre. Their final velocity showed a correlation with the mass of the Galaxy.

There are two possible explanations used to explain this conundrum.

There are only two possibilities. Either GR is right or GR is wrong.

If GR is right, then the inward pull needed to keep these stars in place is so much that a huge amount of extra gravity is necessary. This is much more than the visible components of the Galaxy. So, according to this hypothesis, GR is right and Gravity behaves exactly the way it behaves here. However, there is much more "Dark" stuff out there which interacts minimally with light and its interactions with other fundamental forces of nature are also minimal. It interacts only with the force of Gravity. It is presumed that there is a huge disc of this unique unknown substance called "Dark matter' which lies well beyond the peripheral stars and the arms of the spiral galaxy. There have been several failed attempts to detect these elusive Dark Matter particles. Another ugly aspect of the theory is that scientists must pick the right quantity of this Dark stuff and place it appropriately to explain the data. A theory which requires so many assumptions is usually a bad one.

Contrary to that, the theory of MOND (Modified Newtonian Dynamics) says that GR or Newtonian Gravity doesn't hold at such long distances and that at such long distances or low accelerations, the Gravity reduces proportional to the distance instead of the square of the distance. It however does not give any explanation as to why the well-tested Newtonian dynamics or GR just falls apart at these great distances or low accelerations. MOND needs very few assumptions and the predicted velocities match well with the data for most Galaxies. There are still many discrepancies or inconsistencies and thus MOND is not the favoured hypothesis by most Physicists or Cosmologists. Although science is not a democracy, the majority of Physicists and Cosmologists support the Dark matter hypothesis as it does not need modification of existing laws.

When I read about MOND and its triumphs, I was attracted towards it. The dark matter hypothesis, due to its poor prediction capacity, was not one of my favourite ones.

I came across MOND and drifted towards it progressively since the DGR predicted something similar.

I was wondering what Dynamic General Relativity would predict at such extreme distances.

Every particle of the Sun has extreme energy within, which causes constant destruction of the PCs, I thought. The concentric spherical PC aggregates moving inwards would provide enough inwards pull for the planets to stay in orbit. This actively contracting space would explain Gravitational time dilation as well. But what will happen to a Cubical area made of n PC aggregates? As the space beneath it towards the Sun actively contracts, the Cube moves inwards. During this inward movement, the innermost PC aggregate (EPCA) undergoes more horizontal volume contraction as the Cube moves progressively inwards. Thus, the Cube would get distorted and the outer face of the cube (the one facing away from the sun) would remain bigger. This difference between the outer and inner faces of the Cube is called a tidal force. Essentially, the horizontal spatial contraction would be due to the loss of PCs, but the vertical contraction would be due to the shifting of the Cube inwards.

The horizontal spatial contraction would delay the photon clocks ticking, thus causing gravitational time dilation. As we move away from the Sun or for that matter any source of Gravity, the extent of horizontal spatial contraction will keep reducing until the point where there is no horizontal spatial contraction. At this point, the Gravitational time dilation would become zero or would probably go below 1 Planck time i.e. lose significance. I called this the Gravitational limit of a body. Beyond this distance, the Gravitational time dilation caused by the mass of the body goes in "Sub-Planck-time" zone i.e. the body causes "Sub-Planck-time" time dilation.

What would happen to the PC aggregates and the above Cube when it is in this zone?

The curved EPCAs are probably replaced by the straight EPCAs wherein there is just shifting of the "straight" i.e. "not curved" PC aggregates. This would carry on to infinity or until it approaches the edge of the Universe.

MONDian bonds

The "Sub-Planck-time" Gravitational time dilation got me thinking.

If a star's mass can cause "Sub-Planck time Gravitational time dilation", can the sub-Planck time gravitational time dilations caused by different stars get added up and become significant again? What will be the effect?

More importantly, if we are talking of millions or billions of Sub-Planck time Gravitational time dilations being added together, can its addition exceed 1 Planck time, thus causing actual Gravitational time dilation? From a different perspective, can the straight EPCAs from different stars add together?

Logically, it would be maximal at the line joining two stars.

The theory was hinting at an arrangement akin to carbon atoms in a "mega diamond molecule" where each carbon atom is bonded to four other carbon atoms. So, the outer part of the Galaxy will have all the stars bonded to each other by linear bonds due to the addition of these Straight EPCAs at strategic lines joining the stars.

These MOND bonds would be present even between Galaxy clusters thus explaining E-MOND or extended MOND.

To note is that in the region where the Gravity of the Star causes straight EPCAs instead of curved EPCAs, the horizontal contraction is no longer there and only the vertical component of the contraction in the form of shifting of the EPCAs is present, although with a constant acceleration of a_0.

What this means is that beyond this point, Gravity of the object in question, instead of producing a gradually reducing acceleration will produce a constant but extremely low acceleration. This is applicable for any distance beyond this Gravitational limit. This essentially means that a gravitationally active body, say the Sun exerts the force of gravity according to Newtons laws up to its Gravitational limit and can have a sizeable effect at any distance beyond this including up to the edge of the Universe. One can call this Gravity beyond the Gravitational limit as MONDian gravity.

Mach's principle

There were tremendous implications of this throughout the Universe.

The Gravitational constant "G" is a very small number and thus reduces the overall Gravitational pull of the two gravitating objects.

Could it be caused by the outward MONDian pull of the straight EPCAs from the mass of the rest of the Universe?

This is the same as Mach's principle which states that "mass distribution of the rest of the Universe can exert an outward-directed force on a rotating body (like the Newton's bucket) leading to inertial force that is also called the centripetal force."

The concept of variable G i.e. a different value of G at the periphery of the Universe or a different G at the earlier times in the age of the Universe became possible as described by the "Large Number Hypothesis" described by Paul Dirac.

Central supermassive black holes at the centre of all Galaxies

Almost all Galaxies have a central supermassive Black hole (SMBH). Their mass is remarkably found to be directly proportional to the overall mass of the Galaxy. The larger the Galaxy, the larger the apparent mass of the SMBH. If these straight EPCAs are true, then These SMBH may be just a manifestation of the MONDian gravity of the mass of the entire Galaxy and there may be nothing there but the addition of effects of these straight EPCAs from all the surrounding stars.

Reconciliation of QM and GR

In Dynamic General Relativity, following the successful derivation of General Relativity, Special Relativity and Newtonian Mechanics, I was motivated enough to attempt the reconciliation of Quantum Mechanics and General Relativity. For this, the first hurdle was to derive a description of the Quantum particles like the Electron as per Dynamic General Relativity. It was clear that I had to start with Classical Electromagnetism and go towards Quantum Mechanics later once I had a relatively simple and working model of how classical electrodynamics works in Dynamic General Relativity. The forces involved were different than Gravity. Also here, we needed attractive and repulsive forces. It was clear that wherever repulsion was seen, active creation would be happening between the repelling particles (e.g. Two particles with the same charge) while wherever attraction was seen during experiments, active destruction must be happening in between the two attracting particles. It was clear that there would be no reason to believe the repulsion would happen at the entire space in between and more likely was that there are corridors of active destruction or expansion. Here I came across the problem of "Matter – antimatter asymmetry" that baffled current Physicists. Antimatter basically means particles with negative energy. Physics says that there should be equal amounts of matter and antimatter. But we can only find matter particles with positive energy. Where did all the antimatter go? Here I came across the work of the brilliant physicist Paul Dirac, especially his description of an electron with a negative energy. How I arrived at the current model of the atom is a long topic in itself and involves understanding Spinors and spin and symmetries and cannot be included here.

But it was clear that the Electron or any charged particle must have a reservoir of positive and negative energy.

I also came across the work of Bondi et al and their description of negative mass and positive mass particles.

It was pretty logical that the positive mass would mean destruction and the negative mass would mean creation. I soon internalised that miniature positive mass particles where the destruction of Planck Compartments is happening at their centre would come together and form aggregations. While the negative mass particles, where a PC is formed every Planck time, would keep repelling each other and would never come together. This behaviour wasn't similar to the way the charges behaved. The behaviour of these hypothetical negative mass particles was so weird that when one such particle interacts with a positive energy particle, it would end up in perpetual motion with the negative mass particle perpetually pushing its partner away while the positive mass partner pulling it towards itself. Describing all these with active destruction or creation at the centre and concentric spheres of reactionary compensation by surrounding PCs wasn't difficult in our model. I called them PEPs (positive energy particles – where active destruction of 1 PC per 1 Planck time is happening) and NEPs (Negative energy particles – where active creation of 1 PC per 1 Planck time is happening)

So, the model of electron emerging from Dynamic General Relativity was that there is a high-density positive energy core (PEP core) where constant destruction is happening that corresponds to the observed mass of the electron. The compensation for this destruction forms a reactionary wave that spirals outwards. The negative energy particles form a lattice around and stay separate causing incessant creation within and creating compensatory waves around them. All these compensatory waves interfere and form a complex "Lotus-like appearance".

The interference of positive energy reactionary waves and negative energy reactionary waves results in thin corridors of extremely rapid spatial expansion and contraction wherever these get added up, which I call push bands or pull bands. These corridors will have zones in between, where the positive and negative energy waves (i.e. waves of contracting and expanding space) cancel each other out and lead to zones with zero spatial expansion and contraction in between.

These are snake-like and spiral outwards and form a structure which is structurally, and hopefully mathematically, similar to what is called “the spinor”. Although this was a pretty description and I was pretty proud of it at the start, I soon realised that there were some serious flaws in it. Will the waves not cancel each other out? This would indeed happen if the number of PEPs and NEPs were equal. This description also doesn’t allow for the description of oppositely charged particles. So, what will be the difference between an electron and a positron? I thought.

The solution to it wasn’t far. I just needed to introduce a minor mismatch between positive and negative energy. For this, I assumed that a negatively charged particle presumably has a higher proportion of NEPs and a positively charged particle has a higher proportion of PEPs. This would leave a minor “hole” or “crowding” in the Lattice. This minor change would make the structure unstable and would start reverberating and rotating. I knew that because the electrons were either right-handed or left-handed, they must have distinctly different poles. One of the poles would be the “NEP-excess” pole and the other would be the “NEP-deficient” pole. The shifting of poles would change the handedness. All this explained the handedness of the electrons, spin and even superposition of spin.

Although Physics-wise this model was a triumph, a bigger elation to me was the Vedic description.

Comparing GR with DGR

Comparing GR with DGR

Although the two are completely different and have major implications, they resemble each other closely.

In General Relativity, there is no fixed background coordinate system and no universally progressing forward entity of time – i.e. there is no universal simultaneity. There is no explanation as to why the time is variable. The space in GR is an active player and can bend under the influence of "tensors of Gravity". The coordinate system in GR has no fixed length and thus a cm can contract or expand.

In contrast, Quantum mechanics has a steady unchanging entity of time and an unchanging background coordinate system. So, in Quantum Mechanics there is a definite 1 cm and a definite 1 second. The length of 1 cm and the duration of 1 second is the same everywhere in the Universe. The forces are carried from one place to another by force-carrying particles and the Space does not take any active role in the events i.e. it is a background entity.

DGR on the other hand is a mixture of both. It has a universally static unchanging background coordinate system for which a length of 1 cm is the same throughout the Universe. This unchanging coordinate system is that of the

Field of Nothingness. Superimposed on this, is an actively changing coordinate system where the length of a cm varies due to the creation or destruction of PCs within.

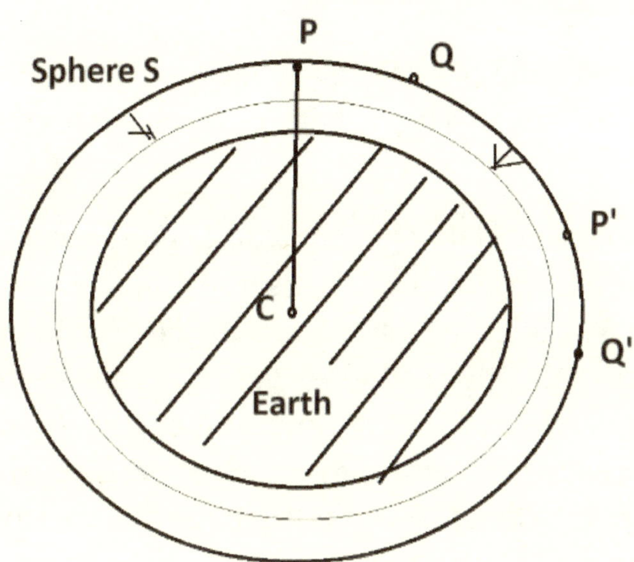

Figure: Shows the Earth with the centre C with a Point P at a distance h from the centre. Drawing the space-time changes that happen due to the Earth's gravity at P is a big conundrum with GR. But DGR would predict that P as well as all the other points like Q, P', Q' etc shown in the figure which form a part of a Sphere S, move inwards i.e. fall downwards towards the centre.

There is a universally forward progressing entity of Time that has an unchanging 1 second everywhere in the Universe that Einstein called T_0. Superimposed on this is the changing entity of time for which 1 second can dilate or contract compared to Universal time and is dependent on the status of expansion or contraction of space in that region. So, the space is in a way married to time. Thus, the theory, unlike GR, provides an explanation for the "gravitational time dilation" or "time dilation due to motion".

To understand the difference between DGR and GR, let's consider the fate of a point P at a distance h from the Earth's centre.

There is a variable opinion regarding the exact shape of space-time distortion that occurs at P due to Earth's gravity in General Relativity. Physicists are unable to draw the space-time distortion. The commonly cited but significantly wrong example of trampoline suggests that the space-time changes are static with respect to time i.e. they do not evolve or change with respect to time. This is far from true and the truth is that even General Relativity predicts dynamically evolving space-time changes. A gravitational wave starts from the Earth and travels with the speed of light causing the distortion. However, there indeed would not be a single wave but multiple waves that keep arriving as time goes forward. With every new wave arriving at P, there will be a change in the position of P. But Physicists reject the idea that GR says that the sky is falling i.e. the point P keeps flowing downwards as the distortion of space at distance h remains constant. DGR, on the contrary, predicts that the point P or for that matter every point around the Earth keeps moving downwards. This "space-flowing" version of a theory of gravity, often called a flowing river type of Gravity is usually dismissed as invalid when describing predictions of GR.

The fate of P in GR is thus a "slight movement which cannot be drawn precisely" as per GR but keeps evolving. In contrast, P keeps "falling" like the apple in DGR. This applies to all the other points around any gravitationally active body like Q.

The fate of the line PQ is also interesting. I don't know what GR predicts will happen to PQ and how it evolves with the passage of (universal) time, although there is no Universal time in GR so such a prediction is impossible in GR, I think. DGR would predict that the length of PQ keeps reducing, and so is all the other potential lines P'Q', P"Q" etc where all these points are at a distance h from the centre. Each of these points in DGR is a single PC and DGR predicts that all these points form a part of a spherical PC aggregate called EPCA. This sphere would keep reducing in surface area and would keep moving inwards eventually touching the surface.

Deriving DGR:

The entire confusion regarding General Relativity and the Newtonian apple or shape of space-time changes around the point P, I think, is because of the inability to understand time and the complete dismissal of Universal time by Special Relativity, the predecessor of GR.

In my opinion, the currently accepted form of GR, with no Universal time, with a tendency to sway towards Block time and with no universal background coordinate system for length, is impossible or not logical. The only form of GR which is logical is the one with dynamically evolving space which boils down to DGR. Although the indivisibility of Space beyond 1 Planck volume is not necessary, it is suggested that to further divide the space, one needs energy (photon) of smaller amplitude, but a photon with such high frequency would inevitably focus energy so much as to form a black hole. So, there is a reason completely unrelated to GR or DGR for assuming atom equivalents of space i.e. Planck Compartments.

So, a line cannot be divided into a smaller volume than a PC i.e. a point represents a PC. Let us attempt a short derivation with these two assumptions.

Derivation:

Imagine any strong Gravitationally active body B (a Galaxy or a Galaxy cluster or the Sun) and two points P and Q at a distance h from the centre of B. They form a part of the sphere S which is an aggregate of a huge number of PCs.

Imagine a chain of photons travelling towards P in a direction tangential to S. The paths of these photons bend inwards due to Gravitational lensing as suggested by GR. As point P is in the path of these photons, the location of P also moves inwards.

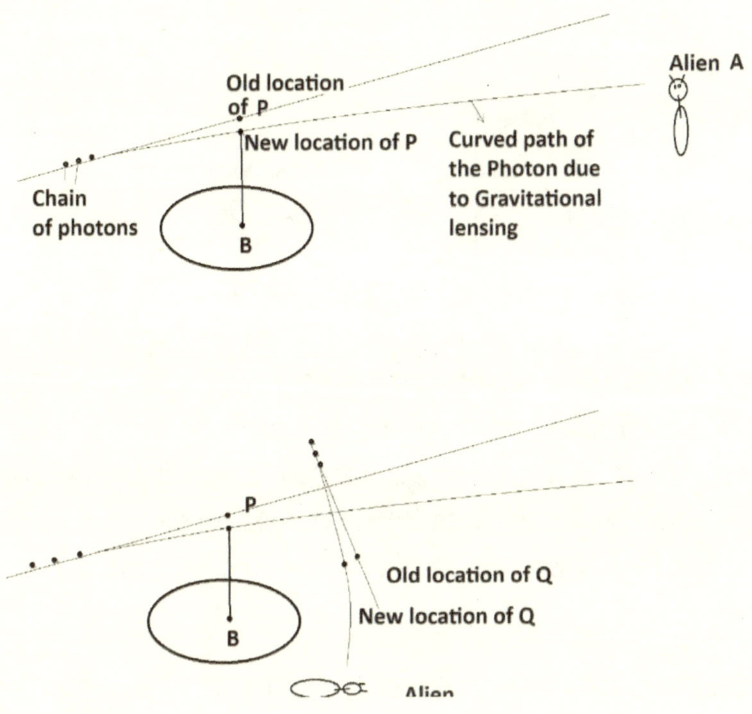

Figure: Shows a gravitationally active body B with a point P. A chain of photons is shown, represented by the three points on the left with their usual path representing the upper line and the slightly bent lower (actual) path due to Gravitational lensing that is detected by a far-away Alien A, shown on the Right side of the picture. Note that the point P moves inwards towards the centre of B. These arguments are valid for any point around B.

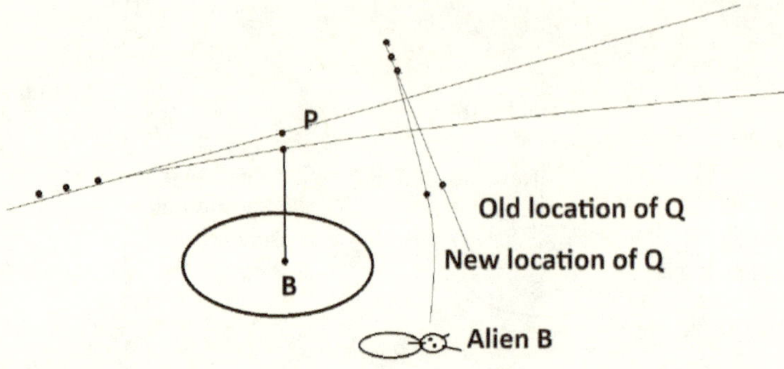

Figure: shows the same gravitationally active body with a similar chain of photons going towards point Q. Note that even the point Q moves downward or towards the centre of B due to Gravity and the gravitational lensing due to this inward movement of Q can be detected by another alien B shown below

Imagine an Alien A, millions of light years away confirming the gravitational lensing with its telescope.

Such a chain of photons can be defined around other points like Q and a different "alien B" can be imagined to detect Gravitational lensing causing a change in the path of these photons by the Gravity of the body B. The same argument applies to the path of these photons, so they bend inwards and thus move Q inward. Thus, P and Q both move inward. These arguments work for any point irrespective of location. So other points on S namely P' and Q' or P'' and Q'' also move inwards. As all of them move towards the centre of B, it is easy to see that the sphere S moves inwards or in the process must lose some PCs simply because each of these lines PQ, P'Q' and P''Q'' lose length as they move inwards.

Another way is to imagine a million drones that are flying at a distance h from the Earth's centre. Imagine that they are moving in a direction and velocity so that they are geostationary i.e. overlying the same point on the surface of the Earth. Each of them drops down a spherical ball. All these balls represent a point in space. All these, fall downwards in a path directed towards the centre of the Earth. Each of them with the same mass will fall with the same velocity and will lie on a sphere. As they drop, the distance between them keeps reducing like the line PQ above.

GR vs DGR

Sr no.	Feature	General Relativity	Dynamic General Relativity
1.	Can explain the Newtonian apple (evolution of space-time changes)?	No	Yes
2.	Can provide explanation for time dilation?	No - it has to be added as an assumption	Yes
3.	Can explain Gravitational lensing?	Yes	Yes
4.	Can explain Tensors phenomenologically?	No	Yes

Sr no.	Feature	General Relativity	Dynamic General Relativity
5.	Number of Assumptions	High	Needs 5 assumptions
6.	At Galaxy scale or above	Needs Dark matter	Doesn't need DM
7.	At entire Universe scale	Needs Inflation to explain uniformity of the Universe	Doesn't need Inflation as light can ride on expanding space and travel faster than speed of light
8.	At a singularity	Breaks down	Doesn't break down due to indivisibility of the space below Planck length
9.	Information loss at Black hole paradox	Exists – cannot explain	No Paradox exists

Sr no.	Feature	General Relativity	Dynamic General Relativity
10.	Twin Paradox	Exists – cannot explain	No Paradox exists
11.	At the scale of Quantum Mechanics	Cannot Reconcile with QM	Can reconcile with QM
12.	Can explain Wave particle duality of light	No	Yes – it can explain
13.	Can explain Wave particle duality of matter	No	Yes – it can explain
14.	Can explain spin	No	Yes – it can explain
15.	Can explain superposition	No	Yes – it can explain
16.	Can explain entanglement	No	Yes – it can explain
17.	Can explain Electromagenetism phenomenologically	No	Yes – it can explain
18.	Can explain electromagnetic bonds and chemistry	No	Yes – it can explain

Sr no.	Feature	General Relativity	Dynamic General Relativity
19.	Can explain MOND	No	Yes – it can explain
20.	Predicts Black hole at the centre of every Galaxy	No	Yes – it can explain
21.	Can derive G mathematically and explain phenomenologically	No	Yes – it can explain
22.	Can explain the weird findings of Double slit experiment	No	Yes – it can explain
23.	Bridge theory between String Theory and Loop Quantum Gravity	No	Yes
24.	Can it Explain Special relativity or constancy of the speed of light	No – it has to be added as an assumption	Yes, it can explain the apparent constancy of c due to

Sr no.	Feature	General Relativity	Dynamic General Relativity
25.	Status of Speed of Light	Constant – follows SR	c is variable in DGR. Still, it doesn't violate SR as the apparent c is still constant despite variable velocity as an increase in velocity is associated with a faster ticking of Local time.

QM vs DGR

Sr no.	Feature	Quantum Mechanics	Dynamic General Relativity
	Can explain Gravitational lensing	No	Yes – it can explain

Sr no.	Feature	Quantum Mechanics	Dynamic General Relativity
	Can explain Gravitational red shift	No	Yes – it can explain
	Can explain Gravitational time dilation	No	Yes – it can explain
	Can explain Super-position phenome-nologically	No	Yes – it can explain
	Can explain weird findings of DSE	Yes, but needs var-ious inter-pretations with no consensus	Yes. Its explanation coincides with the Pilot wave theory
	Can explain why the electron doesn't fall below the first orbit? What provides the repulsive force	No	Yes- it provides an elegant explanation

Sr no.	Feature	Quantum Mechanics	Dynamic General Relativity
	Can explain Quantization of angular momentum	No – it has to be added as an assumption	Yes. It can elegantly explain based on the Push wave going all around the curved space around the central PEP core
	Can it explain Standing wave of the electron	No – it has to be added as an assumption	Yes, it can potentially provide explanation
	Can it explain Matter Antimatter asymmetry	No	Yes, it can potentially provide explanation
	Can it provide explanation for Inertia	No – it has to be added as an assumption	Yes, it can potentially provide explanation

Sr no.	Feature	Quantum Mechanics	Dynamic General Relativity
	Can it provide explanations for Relativistic mass – increase in mass due to motion – especially motion close to the speed of light	No – it has to be added as an assumption	Yes, it can potentially provide explanation
	Can it provide explanations for Higgs field	No – it has to be added as an assumption	Yes, it can potentially provide explanation
	Can it provide explanations for Momentum – Newtons laws of motion	No – it has to be added as an assumption	Yes, it can potentially provide explanation

DGR the "Theory of Everything" in short

DGR the "Theory of Everything" in short

In this section, I will try to explain the theory in short for those in a hurry. The beauty of this theory of DGR is that it can be understood even by kids. Just that it would be difficult in this section to discuss in detail how I arrived at it or detailed phenomenological explanations. A small attempt to give an account of this is tried in the previous section although anyone interested in knowing the details of how the theory of DGR can explain all the currently known physics is referred to my previous book namely "Decoding Gravity Time and Causality". https://notionpress.com/read/decoding-gravity-time-and-causality/hardcover

Or one can subscribe and see videos on DGR at

https://youtu.be/0vkXjcHSZLU?si=ow1Nu5a1aTFDhjUH

The theory of "Dynamic General Relativity" (DGR) as the name suggests is a slightly different form of General relativity. It was described by Einstein in one of his 1911 papers and he called it the VSL type of GR (the Variable speed-of-light type of General Relativity.)

The basic difference between GR and DGR is that in GR, there is a fixed Speed-of-light and a curved space-time while in DGR there is a straight spacetime and a variable Speed-of-light.

It derives some assumptions from Loop Quantum Gravity and Quantum Electrodynamics, eventually leading to concepts similar to vibrating strings. Therefore, it can be said that DGR serves as a bridge theory between LQG and String Theory.

Basic Assumptions

1. ***Space:***

   Space is composed of the smallest indivisible unit known as a Planck Compartment (PC). A PC can be represented as a cube (or sphere) with a volume of one Planck volume, where each side of the cube measures one Planck length (approximately 10^{-35} meters). These PCs are arranged together to form the entire universe and can shift their positions like pieces in a block puzzle. Between any two PCs exists true nothingness, referred to as the PC vacuum.

2. ***Time:***

   There are two types of times in DGR.

   Universal time is time which is universally moving forward and has no effect on the status of expansion or contraction of space at a point. Usually, the time is measured in Planck units of time i.e. 1 Planck time which is 10^{-43} seconds.

Local time is the time that we measure and is intricately linked to the status of spatial contraction or expansion at a point.

3. ***Processes:***

Three processes are taking place – Destruction of PCs, Creation of PCs and Compensation of void created due to these two processes.

4. ***Energy:***

In DGR, energy is of two types: Positive energy is equivalent to active Destruction of PCs. Negative energy would then be equivalent to the active Creation of PCs.

5. *PEP:*

A positive energy particle (PEP) would be the most basic or smallest unit of positive energy. At a point where one Positive energy particle exists, 1 PC is destroyed in 1 Planck time, a PEP is said to exist. This means that at the point where the PEP exists, space equivalent to 10^{43} PCs (i.e. more than 1 meter cube) would be destroyed. So much void needs to be filled in by the surrounding PCs.

6. ***NEP:***

A negative energy particle would be the most basic or smallest unit of Negative energy. At a point where one Negative energy particle exists, 1 PC is being created from nothingness in 1 Planck time. This means that a volume equivalent to 10^{43} PCs is being created every second and leads to the pushing of the surrounding PCs leading to the formation of a significant Void or PC vacuum.

7. ***The "no PC vacuum allowed" assumption:***

   This assumption is inevitable. It is assumed that in between any two PCs, there exists a space called a PC vacuum, which keeps the PCs together. If one tries to separate the PCs, they are glued together. Any attempt to separate them or create a void or PC vacuum leads to compensatory changes in the surrounding PCs to fill the void immediately.

   This assumption suggests that wherever active destruction occurs, the surrounding Planck Compartments (PCs) would be arranged into layers that are one PC thick. These layers then experience active destruction that reduces their volume, allowing the sphere of surrounding PCs to move inward and fill the resulting void immediately.

   Whenever there is active creation of PCs, the surrounding PCs are pushed apart, leading to a void that is compensated by additional creation.

8. ***Time dilation:***

   Around a PEP, active contraction is needed for compensation which leads to the reduced ticking of a Photon clock. Thus, wherever there is active spatial contraction, there is time dilation (as explained in some detail elsewhere in this book during the discussion of the Photon Clock). At the core of the PEP, local time is equal to zero, although Universal time goes on at the usual pace.

In general, wherever there is active spatial contraction, there is dilation of the local time.

9. ***Time contraction:***

   Around an NEP, active spatial expansion is needed to compensate for the active spatial expansion due to the creation process. Thus, at the core of an NEP and also around it, local time seems to be contracted. This is true for any place with active spatial expansion.

10. ***Compensation process and Time resetting waves:***

    Around the PEPs and the PEP aggregate at the centre of every particle, the compensatory active spatial contraction would be expected. Spatial contraction is equal to time dilation. Thus, active destruction at the core causes local time resetting in the surrounding areas. These "spatial contraction time dilation" waves start from the particle and move outwards like circular waves around a stone thrown on a calm surface of water. These eddy time-resetting waves move outwards at extremely high speeds. Similar spatial-expansion time-contraction" type of time resetting waves start around NEPs and lead to the repulsive character of the NEPs.

11. ***Rate of transfer of information***

    The currently accepted form of General relativity puts a limit to causality. It propounds that no transfer of information can occur faster than the speed of light. GR, however, does not put any limit to the speed at which space can expand or contract or the time interval within which the space or its unit (the Planck Compartment) can respond to the PC vacuum created by the process. The question "How fast can the sphere of PCs immediately adjacent to the PEPs respond to the void created due to destruction at its core?" is still open. However, if they respond with a delay of 1 Planck time, then this will set a limit to the rate at which space can expand or contract. These tardy or lazy PCs would be too slow. More likely is that the smallest unit of time or the present is significantly smaller than 1 Planck time and could be in the range of several orders of magnitude smaller than a Planck time. If this is true, then the PCs respond quickly and the Time resetting waves would travel outward much faster than the speed of light. In this scenario which seems more likely, the "information transfer limit" set by GR would be violated.

12. *Eddy Planck Compartment aggregates or EPCAs*

The compensation process and the creation of Planck vacuum create aggregates of Planck Compartments which are almost perfectly spherical all around the PEPs or NEPs. These can be called EPCAs.

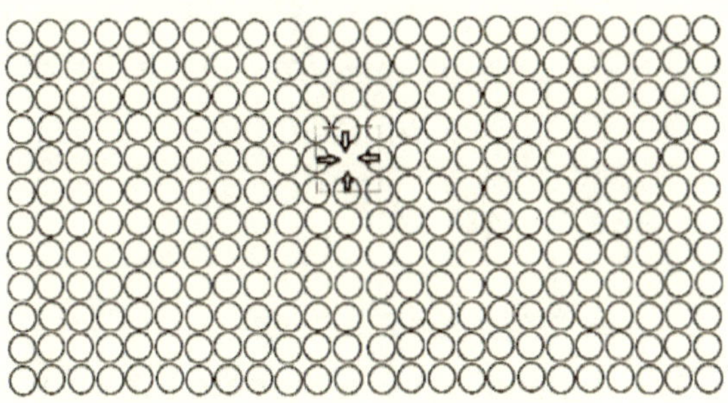

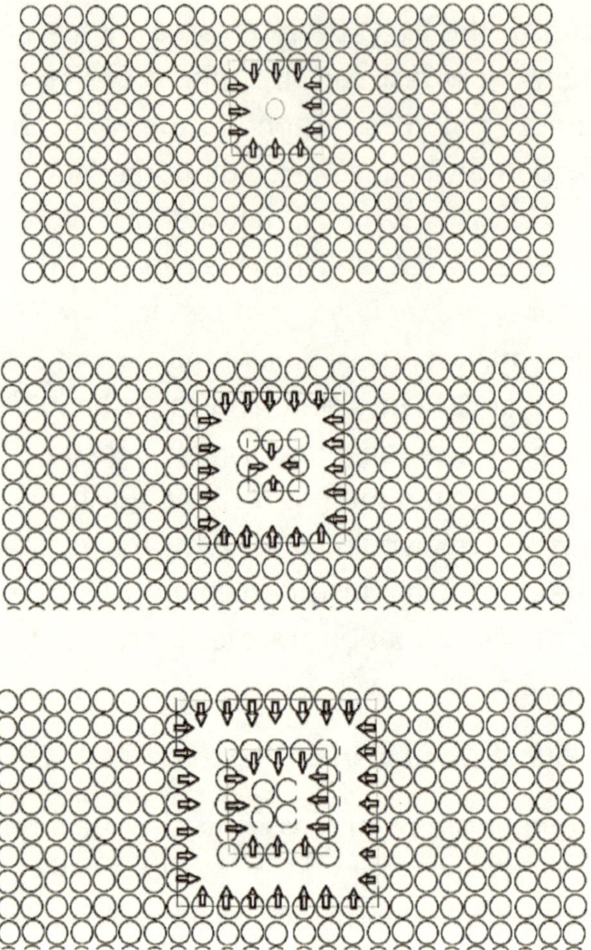

Figure: Shows how Eddy Planck Compartment Aggregates (EPCAs) form around a point where Destruction predominates.

13. *Curved vs Flat EPCAs*

Near the Gravitationally active body like the Earth or the Sun, the EPCAs have a significant curvature. But at extremely large distances like 1-2 light years from the Earth's surface or the Sun's surface, the EPCAs caused due to destruction within the particles that constitute the Earth or the Sun, lose their curvature and become flat. At such distances, there is no horizontal contraction i.e. minimal destruction of PCs that constitute the EPCA.

The only thing happening here is just shifting of level of these EPCAs. At these distances, Newtonian gravity might cease to be effective and MOND may start applying. It is worth noting that the Gravitational time dilation caused by the gravity of the heavenly body in question probably goes below the Planck time scale i.e. becomes insignificant.

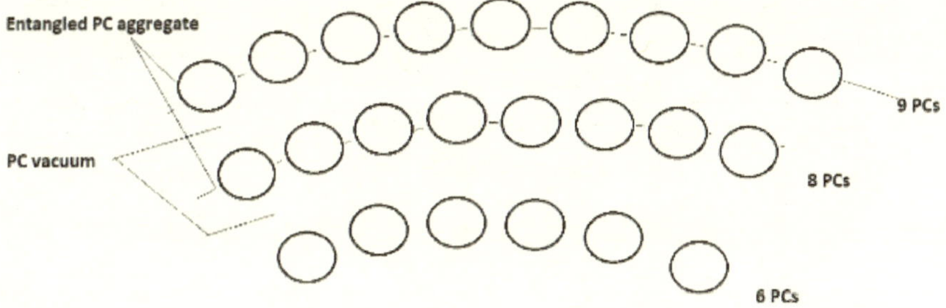

Figure: Shows a spherical/circular EPCA formed around a central point of destruction. Also shown are the various levels where the EPCA would lie in the future as it loses volume and its surface area reduces.

Figure: Shows the formation of a linear EPCA. Here, there is no horizontal volume contraction (i.e. it is negligible). However, there is a shifting of position or level of the EPCA at a relatively constant acceleration.

How is gravity explained in the theory

The falling apple

An explanation of the "Newtonian Falling apple" as a force pulling it downwards given by Newtonian gravity, has been almost completely replaced by the rather difficult to understand concept of "curved space-time of General Relativity". Unfortunately, when you ask the physicists to explain or draw the changes in the curvature of space-time under the apple that makes it fall down, they would find it difficult.

DGR can explain the phenomenology pretty easily. According to DGR, the space beneath the apple, or any freely falling body, is contracting actively and losing volume. "Why can't we see the contraction?" One might ask.

The reason we can experience it but can't see anything is because of the extremely high speed of light. The falling or actively contracting space doesn't cause enough bending of spacetime to produce any deviation detectable by the human eye.

The core of every particle that constitutes the Earth has active destruction of PCs going on within it. This destruction, as explained above, gives rise to compensatory changes in the form of EPCAs. These EPCAs are one PC thick layers. In between these layers, PC vacuum forms and these layers keep descending downwards until they reach the surface. Literally speaking, according to DGR, the sky is falling towards the Earth.

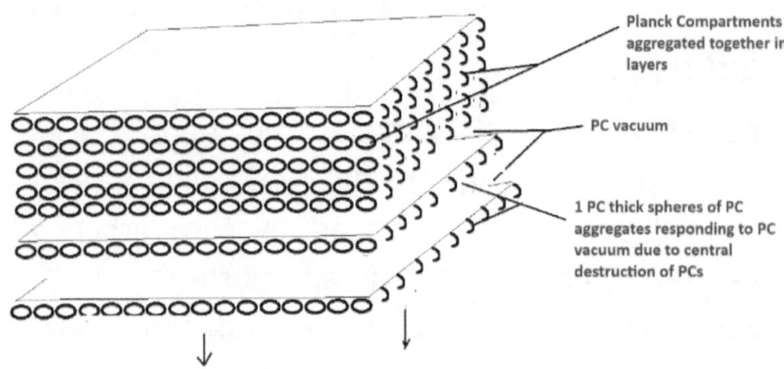

The "Rubber duck floating in a bathtub" analogy

The falling apple can be compared to a rubber duck floating on the water's surface in a bathtub. When the drain is in the closed position and there is no water leaking out, the water level remains constant. But once you open the drain, the water flows out and the water level along with the level of the duck reduces until the duck reaches the bottom. The PCs constituting the space under the freely falling apple are literally being flushed out or destroyed.

How is Electromagnetic bonding explained?

1. ***Interaction between PEPs and NEPs:***

   PEPs have destruction going on within and thus they create compensatory active spatial-contraction type of "time resetting waves" around them. This means that the space around them is in a state of active compensatory contraction. Thus, the PEPs will attract everything else i.e. a PEP attracts both a PEP and an NEP. With other PEPs, it can form aggregates called PEP aggregates. There is no upper limit to how many PEPs can aggregate together.

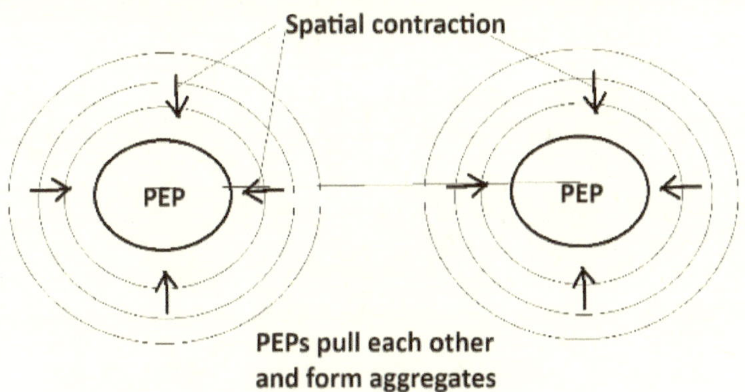

Figure: PEPs attract other PEPs due to actively contracting space around them

NEPs, on the other hand, have active creation of PCs within them and have compensatory active spatial expansion all around them. Thus, the NEPs repel everything. This means that an NEP repels another NEP or a PEP.

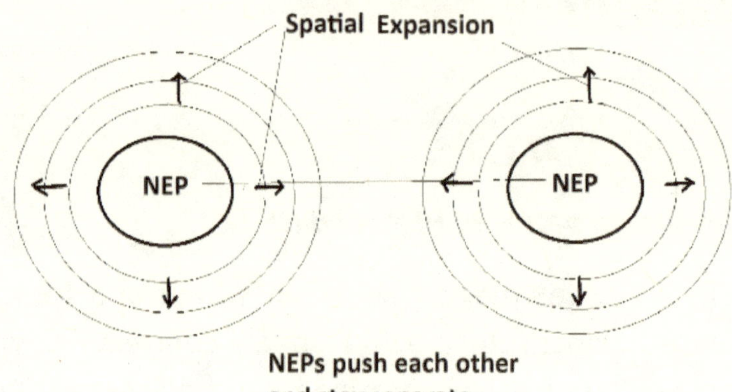

Figure: NEPs repel other NEPs due to expanding space around them

When a NEP approaches a PEP, they enter into a peculiar situation called "Perpetual motion" since the NEP keeps pushing while the PEP keeps pulling.

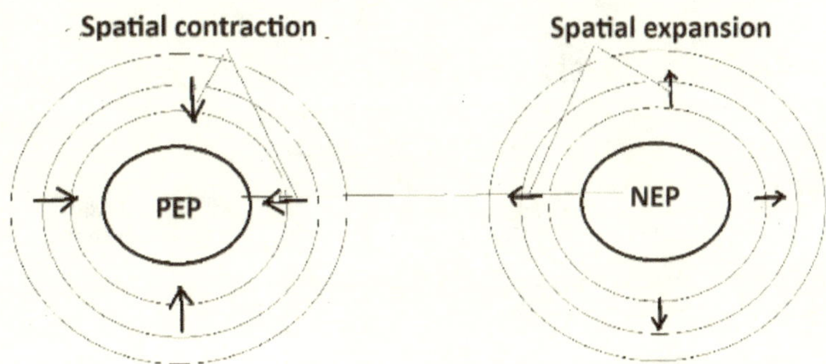

PEP pulls NEP towards itself
NEP pushes PEP away
They enter into perpetual motion

Figure: When a NEP approaches a PEPs, due to expanding space around it, it keeps pushing the PEP away while the PEP is pulling it towards itself due to contracting space around it. Thus, they enter into a peculiar situation called as Perpetual Motion (first described by Bondi et al while describing negative mass)

When multiple PEPs and NEPs come together, the PEPs come together as a central PEP aggregate. The NEPs remain at a distance and form a spherical lattice.

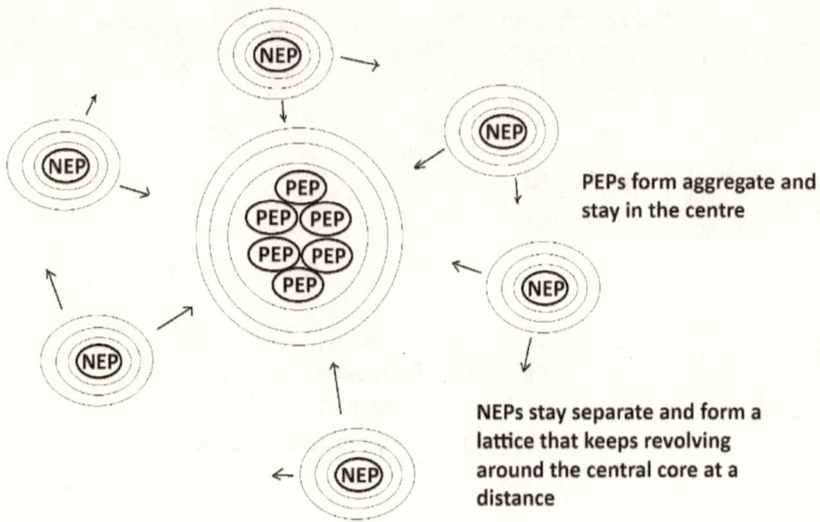

Figure: Shows how Negative energy particles form a lattice around the positive energy core (Diagrammatic)

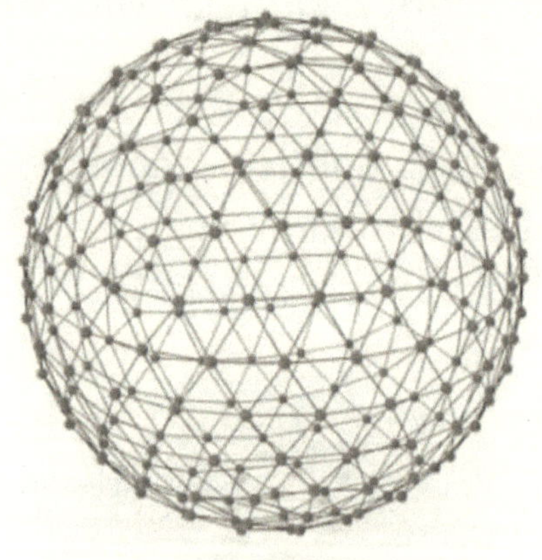

Figure: Shows how Negative energy particles form a lattice around the positive energy core (not shown)

Thus, although they are bonded to the central PEP aggregate, they cannot escape and stay at a distance from the core's centre.

The NEPs stay separate and can't form aggregates.

One can note that with this arrangement, the PEPs and NEPs have a natural tendency to interact and form charged particles as described below.

2. ***A charged particle:***

When an equal number of PEPs or NEPs come together, the PEPs aggregate to the centre and the NEPs form a lattice around it. The compensatory changes cancel each other out and this is the uncharged particle.

It becomes more significant when an unequal number of PEPs and NEPs combine. In this scenario, a deficiency remains in the resulting particle.

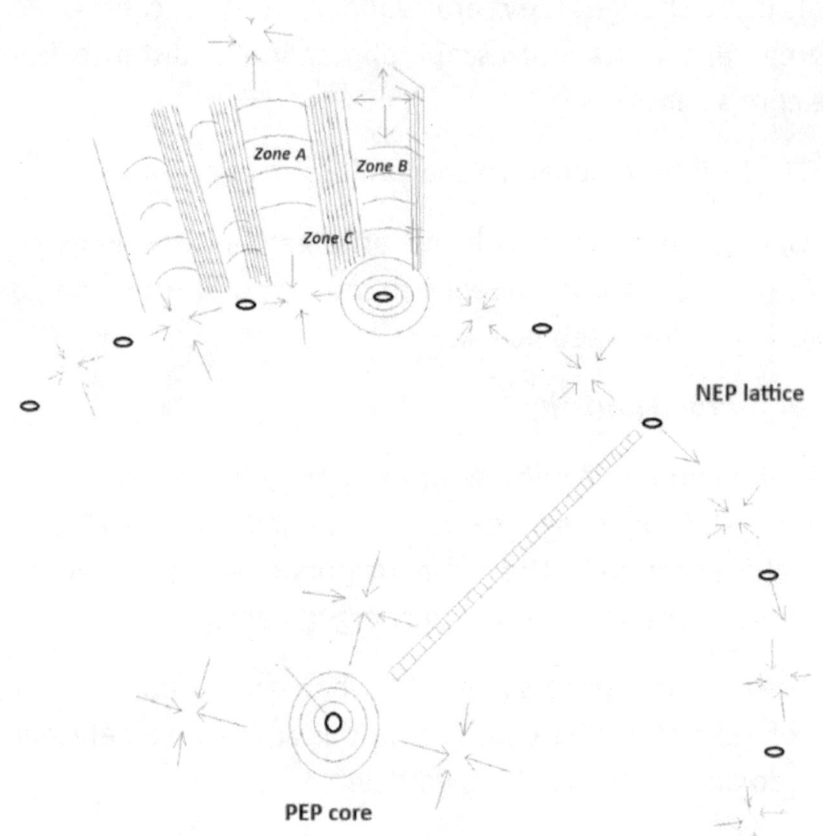

Figure: Shows how a positive energy core will give off "Time dilation spatial contraction" type time resetting waves in the centre and would cause an escalator of PCs being sucked inwards. The lattice is made up of much lesser negative energy each can remain stable at a distance. The zone immediately around the charged particle would be divided into various time zones depending on the Local Time changes. Zone A probably has excessive time dilation and active spatial contraction, zone B has excessive time contraction and thus active spatial expansion and zone C, i.e. intervening zone with no spatial expansion or contraction due to Local time running with Universal Time.

Arbitrarily (as a convention), if there are more PEPs in the core than the NEPs then it is a Positively charged particle like a Positron or Quark. If there are more NEPs in the lattice as compared to the PEPs in the core, then it would form a negatively charged particle like an Electron.

3. ***Compensatory changes around the Charged particle***

With many PEPs aggregated at the centre and NEPs aggregated as a spherical lattice around the central aggregate, the processes of destruction at the centre and active creation at the individual NEPs would keep going relentlessly. These processes lead to compensatory changes in the surrounding space. The time-resetting waves emanating from the core and also from each of these NEPs interact. The complex interaction can be predicted with great accuracy. Details of this cannot be included here, however in short, the surrounding region is divided into various narrow corridors with different status of local time within them.

4. ***Push and Pull bands***

At places, the local time dilation and local time contraction cancel each other out and lead to noncontracting non-expanding regions of space which cannot contribute to any compensation. At other places, narrow regions of space are involved in compensation for the active creation or destruction at the particles leading to a significantly higher rate of active expansion or active contraction of space. The narrow regions where the active expansion of space is occurring can be called push bands. These probably start where the NEPs are in the lattice and move outwards towards infinity. The regions where active contraction of space is taking place can be called pull bands. These emanate from the sieve-like holes in the lattice from where the PCs rush inwards to compensate for the active destruction within. Even these pull bands move outwards towards infinity.

(Note that some of the figures included here are taken from my previous book and are included only for understanding purposes although many details discussed in the previous book are omitted here.)

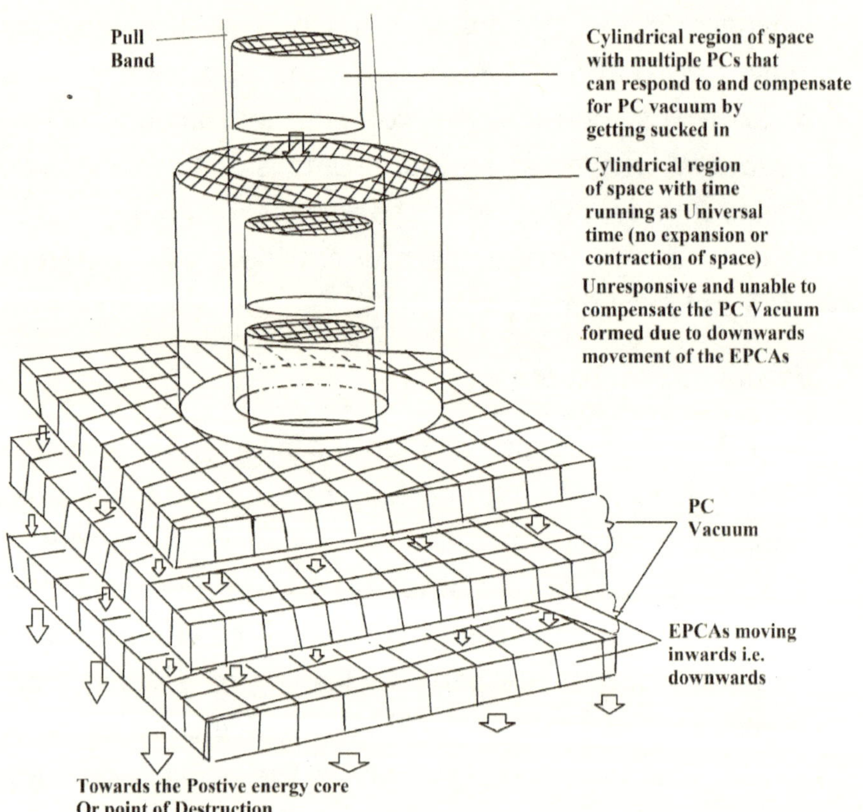

Figure: Shows probable mechanisms underlying the formation of a Pull band. Note that the obliquely shaded cylindrical zone and the uppermost layer of PCs (or 10^6 PC aggregates) have Universal time due to interference between waves from Positive and Negative particles. Thus, they cannot expand or contract, responding to the PC Vacuum developing below the uppermost layer. The Destruction happening at the core leads to the constant development of EPCAs which move inwards causing the constant development of PC vacuum below the uppermost layer. The only way of compensating it is by pulling in PCs from the narrow responsive cylindrical zone which forms the Pull band.

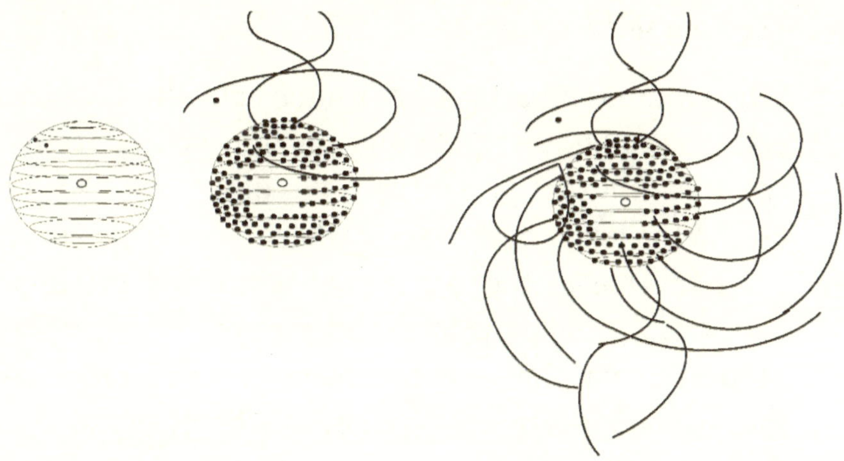

Figure: Shows a diagrammatic representation of a charged particle with a central positive energy core and a peripheral Negative Energy Particles forming a lattice. Note the Push/ Pull bands forming and spiralling outwards. Only some are shown for understanding

5. *Spin of a Charged particle*

The lattice cannot remain static and swings in one direction either anticlockwise or clockwise. Also, there is a mild imbalance in the structure due to an extra PEP or an extra NEP. This creates a small asymmetry so that one pole of the particle differs from the other. One of the poles of the lattice structure would have crowded NEPs (NEP excess pole- EP) and the other would have NEP deficiency with relatively widely placed NEPs (NEP deficient pole-DP). This asymmetry also helps in explaining the direction of spin or handedness of the particle, with two different configurations of spin, right-handed and left-handed.

6. *The Pole shifting*

When there is no external magnetic field, the EP (Excess pole) and the DP (Deficient pole) need not remain constant. Thus, at one instant, the upper one becomes EP and the lower becomes DP while the next instant the poles reverse as the lattice rearranges and the upper becomes DP while the lower becomes EP. The direction of spin remains the same but the poles shift location and thus handedness reverses. Thus, the theory explains the "superposition of spin handedness" effortlessly. When there is an external magnetic field (for example magnetic field created by another interacting charged particle in an atom), the direction of spin and handedness can get stabilised although the lattice cannot remain static and some waxing and waning of the intervening space and local time would still exist.

7. *Electromagnetic interactions and bonding*

The Push bands and Pull bands of one charge can interact with those of another charged particle. If the two interacting particles are of the same charge, the location of push bands coincides and they repel. When they are oppositely charged, the pull bands coincide and they attract. Details can't be discussed here any further.

It's important to note that we are discussing particles with similar masses, such as electrons and positrons. The interactions within an atom occur between protons and electrons, where the masses differ significantly. This theory can also provide insights into the phenomenology behind Quantum Chromodynamics and electromagnetic bonding in chemistry, although those topics cannot be explored in detail here.

The two interacting charged particles within an atom have multiple push-pull bands. The pull bands keep the two oppositely charged particles pulled together. While push bands go all around their partner charged particle and meet on the opposite side to create a standing wave and thus provide the repulsive force needed to prevent the two from falling into each other. This explains many mysteries like atomic orbitals at least partially.

While this concept seems straightforward, the reality is far more complex. In nature, infidelity among bonds is common. The bond between charges within an atom likely lasts only a short period, after which the position of the proton may shift, or the orientation of the interacting charges might change. In the next moment, the electron could bond with another proton and continue this process.

Inner electrons must move within their specific orbits and cannot ascend to a higher orbit without sufficient energy. However, outermost electrons can freely transition between orbits and may even bond with protons from neighbouring atoms in succession, leading to the formation of molecular bonds.

The ultimate aim of the interacting particles is to acquire stability or low energy. The Push band of one interacting with the Pull band of the other leads to stability while the Push band interacting with the Push band or Pull band interacting with the Pull band would be unstable and would apply unrestricted force to the particles and can move the relatively mobile particle significantly.

A static charge also gives off electric and magnetic flux which is the Push-pull bands. These bands form with supra-luminal velocities but drift out with the speed of light. Electrons moving up and down the atomic orbitals form the wave of visible light that enables us to see everything. More energetic EM radiation will have photons which are aggregates of PEPs with destruction happening within but without enough mass to cause significant distortion of the surrounding space.

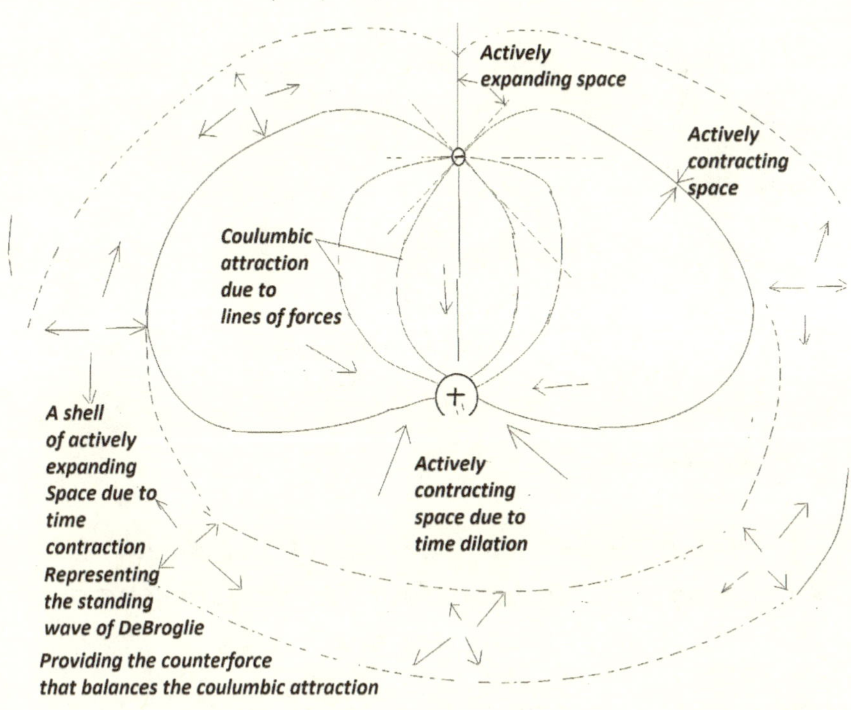

Figure iii/8.1: Shows how the space-time around a positively charged particle bonded with a negatively charged particle might look according to DGR. Especially note the actively contracting space pulling the two particles together and the wave of actively expanding space going all around the positively charged particle providing the repulsive counterforce preventing the particles from coming closer than a limit.

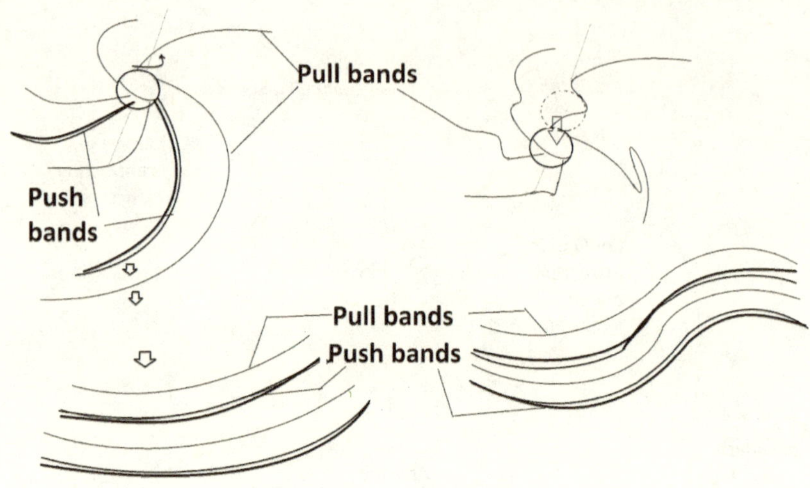

Figure: Shows how the spinning charge with emanating push-pull bands form EM waves/Electric and Magnetic flux.

Note that there is much more to discuss about DGR that cannot be included in this book. The only aim of this section was to give an overview. There are many unanswered questions that require further research.

The Trideva

Srishti is Trigunatmak i.e. with three properties or Gunas

Aims of Writing this book

As I wrestled with my thoughts about this new and unique theory of gravity, I encountered some exciting coincidences. As the theory took shape, I realized that three processes were at work: destruction, creation, and the maintenance of balance.

Wherever destruction of the miniature Planck compartments occurs, the void created is refilled through the process of maintaining balance, which involves additional destruction of the surrounding compartments. Conversely, when the creation of the miniature Planck compartments takes place, the surrounding compartments are pushed away. This results in a void that needs to be filled through further creation.

I was aware of the three Gods or the Trinity in Sanatan Dharma or Hinduism wherein there is a god of Destruction (Shiva), God of Creation (Bramha) and a God of Preservation or maintaining Balance (Vishnu). The Vedas propound that this Srishti (I.e. this universe) is trigunatmak i.e. it has three "gunas" i.e. three properties. I was baffled by the fact that Dynamic General Relativity was in a way also pointing in the same direction. Of the three "gunas," tamas could as well be the Vedic way of saying destruction, rajas could as well be the Vedic way of saying creation and the Sattva could as well be the Vedic way of saying maintaining balance.

The Bhagavad Gita, in the following verse says the same.

Bhagavad Gita: Chapter 14, Verse 5

सत्त्वं रजस्तम इति गुणाः प्रकृतिसम्भवाः |

निबध्नन्ति महाबाहो देहे देहिनमव्ययम् || 5||

sattvaṁ rajas tama iti guṇāḥ prakṛiti-sambhavāḥ

nibandhanti mahā-bāho dehe dehinam avyayam

(Courtesy: https://www.holy-bhagavad-gita.org)

O the mighty/armed one (Arjuna), this prakriti (this material Universe) consists of three *guṇas* (modes)—*sattva* (goodness), *rajas* (passion), and *tamas* (ignorance). These modes bind the eternal soul to the perishable body.

Initially, I gave no heed to these similarities and brushed them under the carpet as "mere coincidence". But soon I realised that so many "similarities" can't really be "co-incidences" and there has to be some underlying truth lying beneath.

A Glimpse of the Trideva - the god of destruction, the god of creation and the god of sustenance or balance

---

One look at the theory and one realizes the extreme co-incidence.

I had made no attempt to insert any of this in Dynamic General Relativity. The theory was an attempt to solve the problems faced by current physics including weird phenomena like superposition, wave-particle duality of light, wave-particle duality of particles, two separate theories for the big and the small, the complete failure of the two theories to reconcile with each other, inability to understand experimental findings like flat rotation curves by GR alone and the need for some unknown particles like dark matter (just to name a few) etc. The aim was never to find similarities between the Vedic teachings, let alone search for the gods.

The three processes of Destruction, Creation and maintaining Balance were not inserted in it but were absolutely necessary for completely delineating the theory. These processes and the theory coming out of them beautifully solve all the problems mentioned above and more (at least in principle). The theory itself has no element of the "Intelligent Creator" or "God" as one of its assumptions or prerequisites and is purely a scientific endeavour.

Is Kshirsagar really "Sea of Cows Milk?"

I had a breakthrough while watching a YouTube video featuring Sadhguru Jaggi Vasudev. He told a tale from the Mahabharata, describing an incident where Kunti called upon the God Vaayu to provide her with a son to ensure an heir for the throne of Hastinapur. During this encounter, the God took Kunti on a ride in a magical chariot.

In the narrative, the Milky Way galaxy was described as something made of "Kshir" or "milk." This prompted me to realize that scriptures often speak in metaphorical terms, and their language should not be interpreted too literally. The "Kshirsaagar," where Vishnu is said to reside, shouldn't be taken as a literal "Ocean of cow-milk." Instead, it can be understood as a metaphorical ocean of milk—representing the milky appearance of the congregation of stars, similar to the Milky Way galaxy.

Whether the interpretation of "Kshirsaagar" as the "Galaxy" we exist within (or as the early universe when only radiation was present everywhere, giving it a white appearance) is accurate remains uncertain. Nonetheless,

I felt compelled to explore alternative interpretations of other aspects of Vedic teachings to find meaning in them.

I kept this "alternative interpretation doctrine" in mind and applied this slightly modified view to other Vedic texts to see if they aligned with Dynamic General Relativity. To my surprise, it worked remarkably well. The "metaphorical" language of the Vedas seemed to echo the principles of Dynamic General Relativity almost perfectly.

Thus, the major aim of writing this book, is to document these baffling coincidences or alternative interpretations and thus document how my theory although absolutely scientific is going remarkably well with the Vedic teachings.

Image 1: Kshirsagar – the metaphorical Ocean of Milk, the abode of Shri Hari Vishnu

Shri Hari Vishnu

Vishnu – (The God of Preservation Protection and Balance) lies on the Sheshnaag, a powerful snake with many heads floating on the Kshirsagar (Ocean of milk)

Vishnu the ***God of Preservation***, is often depicted sleeping or lying down on a large multi-headed snake called ***Shesh Naag***. The Shesh naag is often shown floating in the Ocean of milk with a Shiva linga by his side.

Shankh i.e. a sea shell is often considered a symbol of Vishnu and he is often shown with four arms (Chaturbhuj), one of which is holding the ***Shankh***.

In one of his hands, on the fingers, he holds the ***Sudarshan Chakra*** which is the weapon often associated with Vishnu.

In our theory, the process of compensation often lies among the Snake-like push-pull bands. These push-pull bands are probably several orders of magnitude more powerful than Gravity and are responsible for all the electromagnetic bonding. They are in essence caused due to the compensatory process due to the surrounding PCs reacting to the Creation happening at the NEPs forming the lattice at the periphery of the charged particle and the Destruction at the PEP aggregate at the centre. Thus, this "Vishnu lies on the Powerful snake with multiple heads" makes good sense.

Vishnu and the lotus

शान्ता कारं भुजग शयनं पद्म नाभं सुरेशम्

विश्वा धारं गगन सदृशं मेघ वर्णं शुभाङ्गम् ।

लक्ष्मी कान्तं कमल नयनं योगिभिर्ध्या नगम्यम्

वन्दे विष्णुं भव भय हरं सर्वलोकैक नाथम् ॥

(Courtesy: https://www.stotra.in/translation/en/sri-vishnu/shantakaram-bhujagashayanam)

shāntā kāraṁ bhujaga shayanaṁ padmanābhaṁ sureshaṁ

vishvāa dhāaraṁ gagana sadrushaṁ megha varnnaṁ śhubha anggaṁ |

lakshmīkāantaṁ kamalanayanaṁ yogi bhir dhyāana gamyaṁ

vande vishñuṁ bhava bhaya haraṁ sarvalokaika nāthaṁ ||

Meaning

"I offer my obeisance to Lord Vishnu,

who has a serene and composed appearance, who rests upon the serpent bed (Shesha Naga), and from whose navel blooms the lotus, who is the ruler of the gods.

He sustains the entire cosmos, pervades everywhere like the sky,

appears with a bluish hue like a monsoon cloud, and possesses a divine form.

He iş the cherished consort of Devi Lakshmi, with eyes resembling lotuses,

and attainable by those who practice yoga. I worship Vishnu,

the remover of all fears in the worlds, the singular sovereign of the entire universe."

Many Vedic verses, like the one given above in Vishnu Sahastranaam, say that Vishnu's body is like a ***petal of a flower or lotus petal*** and his eyes are made like a lotus.

Some of his popular names include ***Kamalnayan*** (the one who has the eyes of a Lotus), ***Padmanabh*** (the one who has a Lotus growing out of his umbilicus.)

Prabhu Shri Ram, one of his avatars, has many verses dedicated to him with reference to lotus petals like the one below which is the second verse of Shri Rama Raksha Stotram where Ram is said to have a greyish (Shyam) complexion like a blue lotus and his eyes are like a lotus.

अथ ध्यानम् ।

ध्यायेदाजानुबाहुं धृतशरधनुषं बद्धपद्मासनस्थं

पीतं वासो वसानं नवकमलदलस्पर्धिनेत्रं प्रसन्नम् ।

वामाङ्कारूढ सीतामुखकमलमिलल्लोचनं नीरदाभं

नानालङ्कारदीप्तं दधतमुरुजटामण्डनं रामचन्द्रम् ॥

इति ध्यानम् ॥

(Courtesy: https://shlokam.org/ramarakshastotram/)

---

atha dhyānaṁ

dhyāyed ajanu bāhuṁ drutha shara dhanushaṁ badha padmāsanasthaṁ,

peethaṁ vāso avasānaṁ nava kamala dala spardhi nethraṁ, prasannaṁ,

vāmāng āruda Sitā mukha kamala milalochanam neeradhābhaṁ,

nā nāa alankara deepthaṁ da dhdha tha muru jatāa mandalaṁ rama chandraṁ

iti dhyanaṁ

"One should focus their meditation on Lord Ramachandra, whose arms extend down to his knees, who holds a bow and quiver of arrows, and who sits in a lotus posture. He wears

garments of yellow, and his eyes rival the petals of a freshly bloomed lotus. His expression is serene, and his gaze is fixed upon the lotus-like face of Sita, who rests in his left lap. His complexion resembles the dark clouds of the monsoon, and he radiates with various adornments. His hair cascades down to his thighs.

This concludes the meditation."

Sant Tulsidas in the first verse of one of his Bhajans written in his book Vinayak Patrika, named "Shri Ramachandra Kripalubhajaman" or "Shri Ram Stuti" given below, says that

---

श्री रामचन्द्र कृपालु भज मन हरण भव-भय दारुणम् ।

नव-कंज-लोचन कंज-मुख कर-कंज पद-कंजारुणं

Śrīrāmachandra kr̥pālu bhajumana haraṇabhavabhayadāruṇaṁ.

Navakañjalochana kañjamukha karakañja padakañjāruṇaṁ. ||1||

(Courtesy: https://vedicfeed.com/sri-ramachandra-kripalu/)

Meaning:

O mind, seek the grace of the compassionate Ramachandra, who eliminates the deep fears of existence. His eyes resemble newly bloomed lotuses, his face is like a radiant lotus, and his feet are as soft and red as a fresh lotus.

I found the numerous references to the lotus in the Vedic descriptions of Vishnu quite fascinating. However, the underlying meanings of these metaphorical descriptions often left me perplexed.

As mentioned earlier, the model of a charged particle emerges from our theory as a concentration of extreme levels of destruction at its core, surrounded by a lattice of negative energy (representing creation) that both repels and is attracted to the central positive energy. This dynamic creates a substantial void, and the compensatory changes occurring in the surrounding space (made up of PCs) generate positive or negative energy waves. These waves either pull the surrounding space inward to accommodate the destruction at the centre or push it outward to balance the excessive creation in the surrounding lattice. The compensatory contraction of space results in a gradient of local time dilation, while the compensatory expansion of space leads to a gradient of local time contraction.

The interference of these compensatory waves forms a structure reminiscent of a lotus. All these compensatory processes exist on the "snake-like" push-pull bands. The centre of these compensatory changes resembles a "lotus-like" lattice, where "Brahma," the Creator, and his extensive process of creation reside.

It's understandable that this complex process cannot be easily explained to someone unfamiliar with the intricacies of these PC interactions, their creation and destruction, and the associated compensations. It's often simpler to convey these ideas through analogies that the untrained mind can grasp.

Vishnu and Shankh

Many references to the association of Sri Hari Vishnu with shankh or conch can be noted.

The cross section of a Shankh is known to follow a known pattern which is often termed as Fibonacci sequence. This is noted not only in the Conch but in many places in nature including spiral galaxies.

The compensatory waves and the Push-pull bands described in the section above, that spiral outwards, are likely to be arranged in a similar spiral manner.

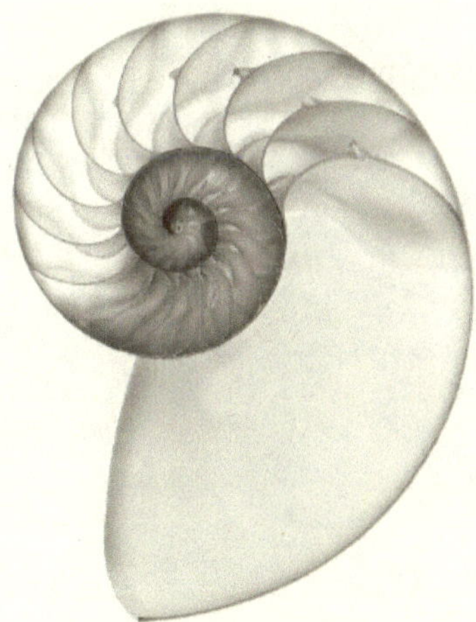

Figure: Shows internal architecture of a Shankh with Fibonacci spiral

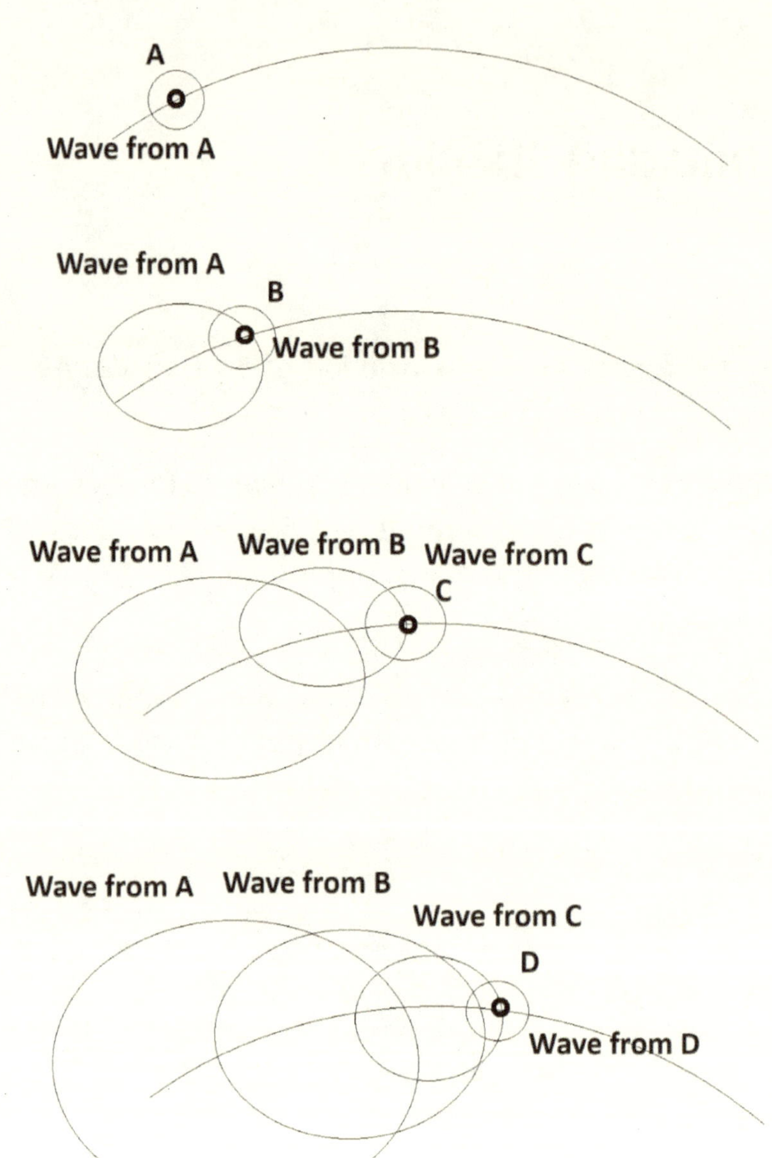

Figure: The four figures show the probable distribution of waves starting from a moving particle as it moves from

different points named A, B, C and D. As the particle moves from A to B, the wave starts from A. As the particle reaches C, a wave starts from B while the wave at A has now become larger. As the particle reaches D, the wave from C starts and waves from A & B have become bigger. This explains how the complex compensatory waves arrange themselves as a Fibonacci spiral

Vishnu is trigunateet i.e. has mastery over all the three gunas

---

There are various stories which describe Shri Hari Vishnu as ***"Trigunateet"*** i.e. beyond the three gunas i.e. has mastery over all three "gunas" or he is in control of all the three gunas. More importantly Shiva and Bramha are specifically mentioned not to be Trigunateet. What this means is unclear, but the "Compensation" process would need to undertake "destruction" wherever needed and "creation" wherever needed. Thus, the "god in control of this preservation process" would need to be able to undertake all three processes i.e. would be a master of all the three "gunas". Thus again, the theory gels well with or seems to be pointing to the Vedic teachings.

Note that the Bhagavad Gita and also the Patanjali Yoga sutras say that we humans get "Vrittis" (impulses) in our "conscious mind" or "Chit". Which Vritti or impulse we get is determined by the "Sanskars" stored in our subconscious mind or "Chitt".

Bhagavad Gita: Chapter 3, Verse 27

प्रकृते: क्रियमाणानि गुणै: कर्माणि सर्वश: |

अहङ्कारविमूढात्मा कर्ताहमिति मन्यते || 27||

prakṛiteḥ kriyamāṇāni guṇaiḥ karmāṇi sarvaśhaḥ

ahankāra-vimūḍhātmā kartāham iti manyate

All activities are carried out by the three modes of material nature. But in ignorance, the soul, deluded by false identification with the body, thinks of itself as the doer.

(Courtesy: https://www.holy-bhagavad-gita.org)

People with predominance of "rajas" get rajasic vritti or impulses common in Rajo Guna like desire, attachment, greed, jealousy, pride, ego, anger etc. People with predominance of "tamas" get tamasic vritti or impulses common in Tamo guna I.e. ignorance (agyan or lack of knowledge), laziness, inactivity or procrastination or fear, divisiveness, enmity, hatred. People with predominance of "Sattva" get sattvic impulses like togetherness, empathy, forgiveness, philanthropy etc. All three gunas are said to exist in every one and thus everyone's behaviour or action (karma) can get influenced by any of these gunas and these actions can have consequences (fala). A person completely under the influence of gunas is like a zombie, completely following emotional impulses. A person not being able to control innate impulses is said to be lacking emotional intelligence. A person completely under control of or not being influenced by these gunas is called “Sthit Pragya” or “Trigunateet”.

The first verse of Rudr Ashtakam says that Shiva is निर्गुणं i.e. unaffected by the three gunas or capable of controlling the three gunas. Thus, one thing is clear, different verses of the Vedic or Puranic literature may be meant for people with different depths of knowledge. The first story of Vishnu being Trigunateet is for those less knowledgeable or Agyani people who want to find a difference between the Trideva, while the verse in Rudr Ashtakam is for people with a higher understanding of the Parabrahma (परब्रम्ह).

The Vishwaroop of Vishnu – all the Trideva are the same

In the Bhagavad Gita, the Vishwaroop of Vishnu is described in a way that suggests a single universal deity known as "Parabrahma" (परब्रम्ह). Vishnu, Shiva, and Brahma are viewed as manifestations of this same deity. This "Parabrahma (परब्रम्ह)" is depicted as having millions of hands, countless in number. This deity has many mouths; one is engaged in "eating" those who die in this world, while another gives birth to all animals and humans.

This deity is responsible for the creation of the "Panchamahabhutas," or the five divine elements that make up the material components of the universe. Parabrahma determines time (Mahakaal) and establishes the laws of nature. It is described that this Parabrahma is omniscient and possesses all the knowledge required to create a universe capable of supporting life. Both living and non-living entities in this universe exist as they do because of this Parabrahma.

In short, this omnipresent omniscient joy-equivalent conscious superhuman all-powerful being is completely free from influence of the three gunas but is the power or force behind the three gunas and controls the three gunas, the aspect of this Parabrahma controlling tamas or destruction is Shiva, the aspect controlling rajas or creation is called Bramha and the aspect controlling the Sattva or compensation is called Vishnu. Although controlling the three gunas, the Parabrahma is nirgun i.e. beyond the effect of the impulses caused by these gunas.

While science often finds the concept of an "Intelligent Creator" at odds with its principles, particularly in the realm of Dynamic General Relativity, it also cannot dismiss the possibility of a universal consciousness or all-powerful being.

The theory requires certain basic assumptions to begin. These assumptions, often referred to as laws of nature by the secular community, are intended to exclude the concept of "God" from the theory. Accepting these assumptions as true is necessary, as there is no underlying theory in the realm of science that explains them.

However, this underlying "theory," which could account for these assumptions, might very well include the idea of a supernatural being. A more scientific approach is to remain open to such possibilities.

Our theory suggests that to actively manipulate or alter the laws of nature, or to allow nature to be non-deterministic, all that is needed is the "active creation of either positive or negative energy at will." The influence of these gunas needs nothing more than active creation of NEPs or PEPs or active creation or destruction happening at specific areas within the brain. It is still hazy and not all answers are known. But the theory can give new direction to finding answers to these questions and help finding this elusive theory of consciousness.

Vishnu resides in this whole Universe

Adobe of Shri Hari Vishnu is said to be Vaikunth or Vishnu Lok. But in one commonly recited tale in Mahabharata, Krishna's mother Yashoda asks him to show what is there in his mouth to check if he is eating butter. When Krishna opens his mouth, Yashoda Maata sees the whole Universe within his mouth. There are many descriptions of Vishnu and Shiva as the owner of the three realms from their names like Triloknath or Trilokadhipati (or Sarvlokaiknatham)

The field of nothingness in the theory of DGR encompassing the whole Universe, and even going beyond this, fits this well.

Bramha

From the umbilicus of Vishnu appeared a lotus within which lies Brahma

The Vedas state that from the naval, or umbilicus, of Shri Hari Vishnu, a lotus emerges, and within this lotus, Brahma, the god of Creation, takes form. A Shiva linga is often showed in close proximity to Vishnu.

In Dynamic General Relativity, the Negative Energy Particles (NEPs), which signify the process of creation, tend to arrange themselves in a lattice positioned away from the central positive energy core, where destruction is continually occurring. The spaces in between these NEPs create spiral zones where compensation for the ongoing processes of destruction and creation takes place, resembling a lotus with many petals.

Brahma has ahankara

Brahma, the god of Creation, possesses a fundamental quality referred to in the Vedas as "Aham" or "Ahankara." This concept means that an individual with excessive ahankara perceives himself as superior or above everyone else. Such a person focuses solely on their own needs and is often indifferent to the needs of others. Consequently, individuals with a strong tendency toward ahankara tend to repel those around them.

The NEPs (Negative Energy Particles) align well with this description. They have a natural inclination to remain separate and will repel other NEPs. As a result, they cannot form aggregates and will also repel PEPs (Positive Energy Particles).

This inherent tendency is fundamental to the theory and is not merely an added assumption. There is a continuous "creation" of PCs (Positive Charges) occurring at each NEP, which causes a push against the surrounding PCs. This push creates a PC Vacuum, leading to additional "compensatory changes" in the PCs in their immediate vicinity.

Surrounding each NEP are spatial expansion waves that reset time. In summary, active spatial expansion occurs within these NEPs at every Planck time, and this expansion repels everything around them.

Image 2: A brass idol of Vishnu lying down on a multi headed snake with a lotus blooming out from his umbilicus with Bramha within it and Shiva lingam by his side.

Image 3: Common depiction of Vishnu lying on a multiheaded snake Sheshnaag, floating in the ocean of milk with Bramha within a lotus arising from umbilicus of Vishnu and Laxmi by the side. Not shown here is the Shiva lingam commonly shown by the side of Vishnu

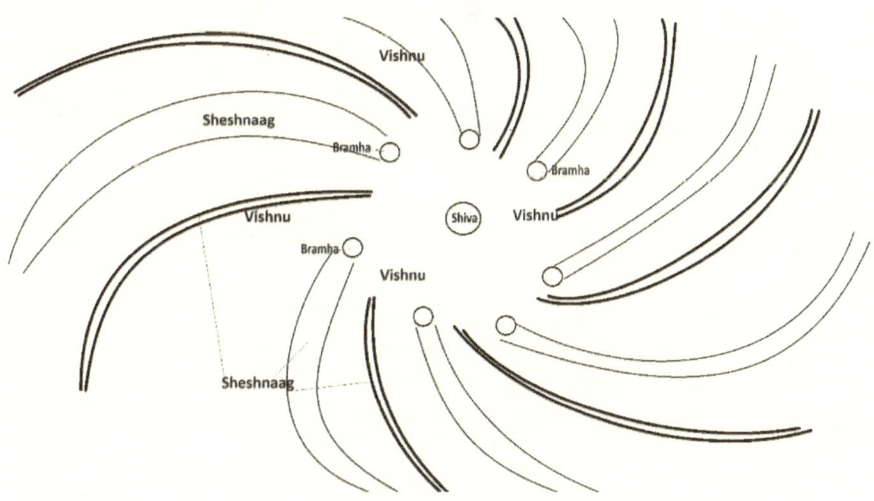

Figure: Shows diagrammatic representation of what the theory of DGR predicts. Shiva is in the centre, Bramha lies in

the lotus-like lattice and Vishnu lies on the snake-like push pull bands. Thus, Sheshnaag is a form of Vishnu, being a result of the compensation process. The various compensation waves which represent Vishnu form a Lotus-like arrangement

Bramha is not worshipped by many due to Ahamkara

There is a folktale that explains how Bramha received a curse due to his "Ahamkara" (also called Aham or Ahankar) or ego/ pride, which prevents him from achieving significance as a deity. Despite being the creator of the entire universe, he is not widely worshipped.

This concept can be seen in DGR without much complexity. The NEPs, representing the process of creation, remain distinct, while the PEPs tend to cluster together.

The PEPs, or Positive Energy Particles, form matter and are primarily responsible for gravity. When aggregated together, they create massive structures in the universe, such as huge stars that can be several hundred times more massive than the Sun, or fiery supermassive black holes at the centres of galaxies, which can exert their influence thousands of light-years away. In contrast, NEPs, or Negative Energy Particles, remain separate and are predicted to be extremely difficult to detect. They do not interact with anything, including light, making them ideal candidates for dark matter.

However, it is not true that they have no significance. Without the NEPs, everything would collapse in on itself, and the Universe as we know it wouldn't exist.

The NEPs provide the most important repulsive force necessary to keep the various particles separate and prevent them from collapsing gravitationally. They prevent the Electron from falling into the Nucleus under their electromagnetic attraction.

Thus, everything has its significance. Bramha is equivalent to the "Parabrahma" i.e. there is a single deity with different manifestations and thus this is not an attempt to show one deity superior to another. The difference we perceive is just due to our ignorance.

Bramha is called as Nirgun

Many verses, including the following, are dedicated to Lord Brahma, the god of Creation in Vedic and Puranic literature. These verses proclaim that Brahma is Nirgun or formless.

ॐ नमस्ते परमं ब्रह्मा,

नमस्ते परमात्मने ।

निर्गुणाय नमस्तुभ्यं,

सदुयाय नमो नमः ।।

om namaste paramam bramhā

namaste paramātmane

nirgunāya namastubhyam

saduyāya namo namāh

Meaning

Om, I bow to the supreme Lord Bramha,

I bow to the highest consciousness.

To the formless, I offer my salutations,

And to the one who embodies the essence of goodness, I offer repeated salutations

---

Given that NEPs represent Bramha and the NEPs remain separate and without the typical form of an Idol which is made of material elements, fits well. But looking from a different perspective, Bramha, on in-depth analysis isn't "Nirgun" i.e. devoid of "gunas" but is the principal deity for "rajas" or "Rajo guna". Another way of thinking about it is that Bramha is in charge of Rajo guna but being Prabrahman is nirgun i.e. unaffected by any gunas. The true meaning remains speculative.

In Vedic literature, the term "Bramhan" or "Brahman" (ब्रम्ह) is often used as "Parabrahma" or the one and only Deity who takes different forms and is thus equivalent to Shri Hari Vishnu, Shiva, and Brahma.

Bramha lives in Bramha lok

Vedic literature suggests that Bramha lives in Bramha Lok, with his consort Saraswati which is far away from Prithvi (the Earth) and it is inaccessible to most humans. Only certain humans with superhuman abilities can make that journey.

In our theory, although Negative energy is present around every particle, the intergalactic regions where the Universe expands, a particularly high density of NEPs exists. Here, the NEPs are so high that anything made up of matter like an intergalactic spaceship entering this region can get ripped apart due to the constant Creation. The theory imposes a limit on how far humans can travel in space, particularly regarding intergalactic travel. Although this may seem discouraging, it is currently impossible for humans to leave the Solar System with our existing technology. Even reaching the edge of our Galaxy is beyond our capabilities, and developing faster-than-light travel would still not suffice, as such a journey would take several thousand years, even at the speed of light.

A day of Bramha is equal to many Yugas

The Vedas indicate that Brahma's time operates differently than ours. One day or night for Brahma is equivalent to 1,000 cycles of the four yugas, totalling 8.64 billion years.

This wasn't completely unexpected to me.

NEPs or Negative energy particles must have active spatial expansion within them. This is essentially hypercontracted time in contrast to the dilated time near a Gravitationally active body due to active spatial contraction (see the discussion on the photon clock) or a hyper-dilated time within a PEP aggregate.

Imagine that one observer is sitting within these NEPs. For this observer, time would run so fast that a minute perceived by him would be equivalent to years on the Earth.

Here, the limitations of the human body and the conscious mind come into play. It remains unclear whether our perception includes a component of time that is completely independent of the surrounding space—essentially an intuition of time—or if our conscious mind compares the perceived speed of time to the environment around us.

If our consciousness compares the faster-ticking photon clock with an intuitive sense of universal time, it may seem to tick faster to us. However, if we lack such an intuition, a conscious being existing in a different hypothetical space within the NEP would perceive its faster-ticking photon clock as normal. From that being's perspective, the photon clock ticking on Earth or the one held by Mahakaal, which shows universal time, would appear to tick more slowly.

For this "NEP-conscious being", his (or her) own time would tick normally, while the clocks of others would seem to tick more slowly.

However, I prefer not to delve into the details of math, as it is exceedingly difficult to understand and the benefit of thinking this way is minimal.

Shiva

Shiva is "the one who is not"

The meaning of the word "Shiva" is the ***"one who is not".***

This description aligns well with our theory, as Shiva represents a void in between the Planck Compartments.

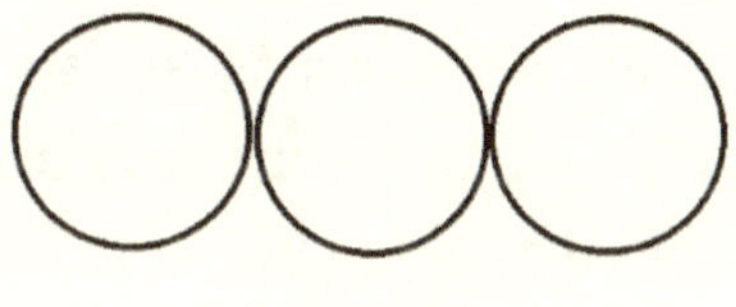

Manifest form
i.e. Planck Compartments that can be represented as "1"

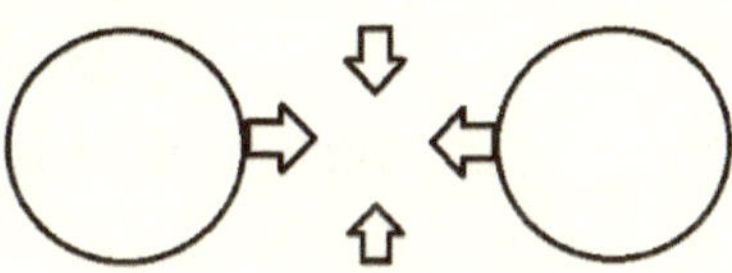

Un-Manifest form
i.e. Planck Vacuum that comes into existence when a PC is destroyed It can be represented as "0"

Figure: All the phenomena happening throughout the Universe can be explained based on just these two aspects of the Universe, the Manifest form and the Unmanifest form.

It is like a true vacuum wherein the two Planck compartments cannot separate. Any attempt to separate them pulls them together or gives rise to the "Compensation" process that leads to additional destruction or creation to compensate for the void. In Einsteinian General Relativity, it is akin to a "Wormhole" or a Blackhole.

Our theory suggests that this Universe is made of two things – 1. A Planck Compartment and 2- A Planck vacuum. This is pretty much in line with the Vedic teaching that this ***"Srishti"*** is made of two things ***"the Purush" (or the Shiva)*** and ***"the Prakriti" (or Shiva's consort "Shakti" or Parvati)***. (Note the similarity between this and the binary code wherein a PC represents 1 and the PC vacuum represents 0 – thus every moment, this universe is rewritten in a binary code thus giving some credibility to the "simulation hypothesis" wherein it is said that we live in a computer simulation.)

In essence, Shiva is "***nothingness***" in between. All the PCs this Universe is made of, have a nothingness in between as a universally present field. What the theory suggests is that just outside the boundaries of this Universe also exists this same nothingness which pulls the boundaries apart and leads to an ever-expanding Universe. Thus, this whole universe is lying within this "Nothingness" of Shiva. This is akin to the Physics theory which says that the whole Universe may be within a Blackhole.

Wherever there exists two Planck Compartments, there is a presence of this Planck vacuum or nothingness in between. This indicates that this nothingness permeates the entire Universe and exists beyond it. This aligns well with the Vedic description of Shiva as Omnipresent or Sarva-vyaapi.

Shiva and Shakti, the Ardhanarishwara form

Understanding Shiva and Shakti (Shiva's consort) can be a complex task. The Ardhanarishwara form of Shiva symbolizes the belief that Shiva and Shakti are one and the same. Additionally, comprehending the concept of Trideva is also quite challenging, as they are believed to have emerged from Shakti.

Shakti is often equated with "energy" instead of Shiva, as mentioned earlier.

At times, Shiva is depicted as Nateshwar or "the actor" and plays the roles of Vishnu or Brahma. In essence, there is a single Deity called "Parabrahma Parameshwar" and all these are just different roles played by the same omnipresent omniscient Deity.

In our theory, this Universe is made up of two aspects, the PC and the PC vacuum as mentioned before. Here the PCs represent the fabric of the Universe or the evident aspect of the Universe including everything material. The word used for this in Vedic literature is "Prakriti".

Image 4: Shows the Ardhanarishwara form of Shiva wherein Prakriti or Parvati is shown as an integral part of Shiva and is left half of Shiva

Shiva is Happiness and Consciousness

Shiva is commonly referred to as "Sat," "Chit," and "Anand." In this context, "Chit" means consciousness, which is distinct from "Chitt," referring to the subconscious mind. "Anand" signifies happiness. The term "Sat" has multiple meanings; it can represent truth, purity, or something that is everlasting and without end. Shiva is also said to be Aj Ajar and Amar i.e. with no beginning, never becoming old and never ending i.e. the one who can never be destroyed.

Consciousness remains a mystery, as no one truly understands what it is. However, if we consider this universally present state of "Nothingness" that represents Shiva as a form of consciousness, it aligns with the theory of "Universal Consciousness" or "Panpsychism."

Similarly, "Anand," or happiness, is a subjective experience characterized by "qualia," which transcends words and is ultimately indescribable. The highest form of happiness, often described in spiritual contexts, is achieved through becoming one with Shiva, known as Moksha.

The four Purusharthas described in the Vedas represent different types of happiness. “Kama” refers to the short-term happiness we experience from physical intimacy, enjoying good music, or savouring delicious food. “Artha” signifies the short- to medium-term happiness derived from material possessions. “Dharma,” on the other hand, relates to the long-term happiness we gain by fulfilling our responsibilities and successfully managing our duties.

Each of these experiences leads to happiness of distinctly different qualities, known as qualia, and is often linked to various neurotransmitters. “Kama” is associated with oxytocin or dopamine, while “Artha” and “Dharma” are connected to serotonin, which creates a more enduring sense of happiness or satisfaction. A deficiency in these neurotransmitters can result in sadness or depression, necessitating their upregulation for treatment. For instance, SSRIs (selective serotonin reuptake inhibitors) are a class of medications that increase serotonin levels, helping to alleviate depression.

However, the underlying reasons behind the impulses that trigger the release of these neurotransmitters in response to certain life events remain unclear, indicating that a “non-materialistic” component may be involved in their release.

Purusharthas are nothing but the four pursuits which a human being is supposed to follow. Although there is much to discuss regarding the Purusharthas and human behaviour, this book is likely not the appropriate venue for such an exploration. Therefore, “Shiva: The Ultimate Universal Consciousness” will not be addressed in significant detail here.

However, it is important to note that a comprehensive and logical ***theory of consciousness*** can be derived from DGR, drawing heavily from the ancient wisdom found in the scriptures. In these texts, the subconscious mind, referred to as "Chitt," serves as a reservoir of tendencies that instil "vrittis," or impulses, in the conscious mind, subsequently influencing individual behaviour. Developing this theory, however, would require considerable effort. A prerequisite would be to give up the compulsion in the scientific mind to have a "Deterministic Universe" wherein everything is pre-decided. One has to also part ways with pure materialism wherein only the brain and materials that we see like neurotransmitters are responsible. Describing the conscious mind within the Brain is easier but deciphering the exact location of the sub-conscious mind within the material Brain becomes an impediment and so does elucidation of the exact location where the "vrittis" or "tendencies" are stored or the mechanism of their reappearance.

One of the famous verses in "Atma Shatakam" written by Shri Adi Shankaracharya, says

---

मनोबुद्ध्यहंकारचित्तानि नाहं

न च श्रोत्रजिह्वे न च घ्राणनेत्रे ॥

न च व्योमभूमिर्न तेजो न वायुः

चिदानन्दरुपः शिवोऽहम् शिवोऽहम्

Man, buddhi ahankāra chittāni nāham

Na cha shrotra jivhe na cha grhāna netre

Na cha vyom bhumih na tejah na vāyuhu

Chit ānand rupah shivoham shivoham shivoham

Courtesy https://isha.sadhguru.org/en/blog/article/nirvana-shatakam-lyrics-meaning)

Meaning:

I am neither the faculties of the mind, such as intellect, ego, or memory,

nor the senses of hearing, taste, smell, or sight.

I am not the elements of space, earth, fire, or air.

I am the essence of pure awareness and bliss; I am Shiva, the formless one.

It tries to answer the troubling question "Who am I" or what is the reality of the "Conscious mind". It simply states that "I am neither mind nor intelligence nor ego. I am Shiva,

I am Shiva, I am Shiva. This simply means that "the conscious entity" or "consciousness" residing within us that can acknowledge that "I am there" is a small portion of this vast ocean of "Aware Nothingness" i.e. Shiva.

The sixth verse of Rudr Ashtakam, repeated again below says that Shiva is सज्जनानन्ददाता i.e. the giver of happiness to the Sajjan i.e. dharmic or good people. It also says that Shiva is a पुरारी i.e enemy of the demons named Tripurasuras due to which Shiva is also called Tripurari. Shiva is also चिदानन्दसंदोह i.e. the one who gives eternal bliss and मोहापहारी i.e. the one who removes worldly entanglements, another word for which is "Moh" or attachments. He is also called मन्मथारी or the destroyer of Kama dev, the God of lust.

कलातीतकल्याण कल्पान्तकारी

सदा सज्जनानन्ददाता पुरारी ।

चिदानन्दसंदोह मोहापहारी

प्रसीद प्रसीद प्रभो मन्मथारी ॥६॥

kalātīta-kalyān-kalpānta-kāri

sada-sajjan-[ā]nanda-dāta-purāri

chidānanda-sandoha-moha-pahāri

prasida-prasida-prabho-manmathāri||6||

(I offer my salutations to Bhagavan Shiva),

who transcends material existence, who strives for the upliftment of others,

who brings an end to the cycle of creation, who grants joy to the virtuous (dharmic individuals),

and who vanquished the demon Tripurasuras (representing adharmic forces),

who eradicates attachments and imparts wisdom to his devotees.

O compassionate one, O compassionate one, destroyer of Kamadeva, please be gracious. ||6||

Tripurasuras represent "adharma" i.e. everything that is against the teachings of Vedas that comes in the way of the ultimate goal of Human life i.e. Moksha i.e. being one with Shiva. Kama Dev is the God of lust. Kama is lust or desire. Although it is one of the Purusharthas, it is also considered one of the Shada Ripu or one of the six enemies of the mind as per the Bhagavad Gita, others being krodh (anger), lobh (greed), moh (attachment), mad (state of arrogance or pride or excessive self-love i.e. ahankara) and matsara (i.e. jealousy). All these tendencies are said to be generated because of the influence of the three gunas. Shiva or consciousness within us can win over all these. The most important hurdle between that is the lack of self-realization. Once the self-realization dawns that the conscious entity within this non-conscious body controlling every function is Shiva and is capable of winning over the effects of these three gunas and thus capable of keeping the harmful effects of these shada ripu away, is said to be the Nirvana i.e. ultimate happiness. So, Shiva is also called as निर्वाणरूपं i.e. the giver of Nirvana or Moksha or ultimate bliss. It would be intriguing if this is true, but it could mean that whenever we are happy, we are experiencing Shiva or coming close to him.

It is clear that Narayana or Shri Hari Vishnu is often called "Buddhi data" i.e. giver of Intelligence and thus wherever we use the word Shiva in the above para, one can easily replace it with Parabrahma or Narayana.

It is also clear that the Conscious agents can subconsciously get an impulse to get angry or they can consciously choose to get angry. The latter involves more cognition and is more energy-consuming. Does this mean that this Soul or Conscious agent within the body is capable of generating all the three gunas within?

It is unclear what these gunas represent, but it is likely that tamas is destruction, rajas is creation and Sattva is maintaining balance. The conscious agent, being capable of manipulating all three gunas, is probably an entity capable of spontaneously producing energy (PEPs or NEPs) at extremely precise locations in the human brain.

After a certain level of expertise, humans are capable of experiencing happiness all by themselves and do not need any external stimuli or good events. (The person capable of feeling happiness irrespective of good or bad events happening around has been named "Sthitapradnya" in the

Bhagavad Gita.) This happens after the self-realization i.e. dawn of understanding that "I" am Shiva.

The feeling of happiness is of a distinct kind and distinct receptors and neurotransmitters are involved as discussed elsewhere including dopamine, oxytocin and serotonin. The quality of happiness perceived by the consciousness with each of these is different. It is unclear whether the release of these is absolutely mandatory for perceiving these kinds of happiness or not although it is likely that the conscious agent within the human brain can derive the information about the release of these neurotransmitters. In essence, it is likely that the Conscious agent is not only capable of producing positive and negative energy but is capable of deriving information from specific regions of the Brain and possibly capable of consciously influencing the release of many neurotransmitters. Conscious or Subconscious impulses influencing the release of many substances like gastrin, cholecystokinin regulating the digestion process, influencing the tone of the lower oesophageal, anal or urinary sphincter leading or heart rate or blood pressure are the probable reasons that stress and sleeplessness can lead to dysregulated digestion and GERD (gastroesophageal reflux disease), constipation and perianal diseases like piles and coronary artery diseases and strokes. These are also the reason why meditation or chanting of mantras/shlokas/bhajans calms the impulses and influence the activity of these chemicals in reducing stress.

Initially, neuroscientists believed that the location of brain stimulation is important for the perception of a type of happiness. Subsequently, the chemistry started becoming clearer. What if we have a model in which the same neurotransmitters are made to release in the brain, but at a different location or the same location of the brain has been designed to get exposed to different neurotransmitters? Will the subjective feeling of happiness change or remain?

Early attempts at neuroscientists implanting a chip in the brain of severely disabled Quadriplegic wheelchair-bound individuals have been promising. It was noted that these individuals can actually learn to manipulate a cursor on the screen and play a game of chess when the wire to the chip is attached to the screen of the computer. Thus, the conscious agent within is capable of generating electrical patterns in the brain that lead to electrical stimulation of the chip in a precise manner to manipulate the cursor. These promising results could mean a potential for these disabled individuals to attain capabilities to control a computerised wheelchair for locomotion or even an artificial exoskeleton suit that can take up their weight and enable them to walk despite no function of the spinal cord below the neck. With a working theory of consciousness with conscious agents with DGR, significant progress is likely in this regard.

Shiva has snakes wrapped around his neck, tiger skin wrapped around his body and has ash smeared over his body

---

Shiva is often depicted wearing a tiger or leopard skin draped around his body, characterized by its stripes. The last line of the fourth verse of Rudr Ashtakam (given below) also describes Shiva as having animal skin wrapped around him (मृगाधीशचर्माम्बरं).

मृगाधीशचर्माम्बरं मुण्डमालं

प्रियं शङ्करं सर्वनाथं भजामि ॥४॥

mrigā-dhisha-charmāṁ -baraṁ -munda-mālaṁ

priyaṁ -shankaraṁ -sarva-nathaṁ -bhajāmi ||4||

(I offer my salutations to Bhagavan Shiva),

He is adorned in garments made from tiger skin and wears a garland of skulls.

I revere the beloved Shankar, the supreme lord of all. ||4||

This "stripped" appearance of the tiger skin resembles the stripped appearance of the Spinor model around the charged particle (see the figure of spinor in coloured images)

Additionally, he is commonly shown with "Vibhuti," or ash, smeared all over him and is depicted with snake named "Vasuki" wound around his neck.

Shiva's description of being smeared with ash was astonishingly similar to the positive energy core, where incessant destruction is happening at the centre of every particle, being covered with the ash of Negative energy particles (NEPs) around it.

Also, the PEP core is surrounded by many snake-like Push Pull bands which can be representing the strips in the tiger skin wrapped around Shiva or the snake around his neck.

In Vedic scriptures, there are some contradictory statements about Shiva. In some texts, he is described as omnipresent (like व्यापकं or "vyapakam" I.e. spread in all directions or all-encompassing as per first verse of Rudr Ashtakam), meaning he is present everywhere. In other instances, it is stated that he exists in every particle (कण कण में or "kan kan mein").

Both these statements make sense since the "field of nothingness" or the "Planck vacuum" is present in between all the Planck compartments and the process of destruction is present incessantly destroying PCs at the centre of every particle.

Image 5: Shows Shiva as commonly described in the Vedas. He has snakes around his neck, wears a tiger skin with stripes, has a trident, has a damru, has the river Ganga flowing out of his matted hair, has ornaments made up of Rudraksh and has a crescent moon on his forehead. Note the three eyes

(Trilochana) and the blue hued throat (Neelakanth). Also note the eternal Bliss radiating from his face and the posture of giving boon suggesting that he is the giver of happiness and giver of boons for the upliftment of everyone.

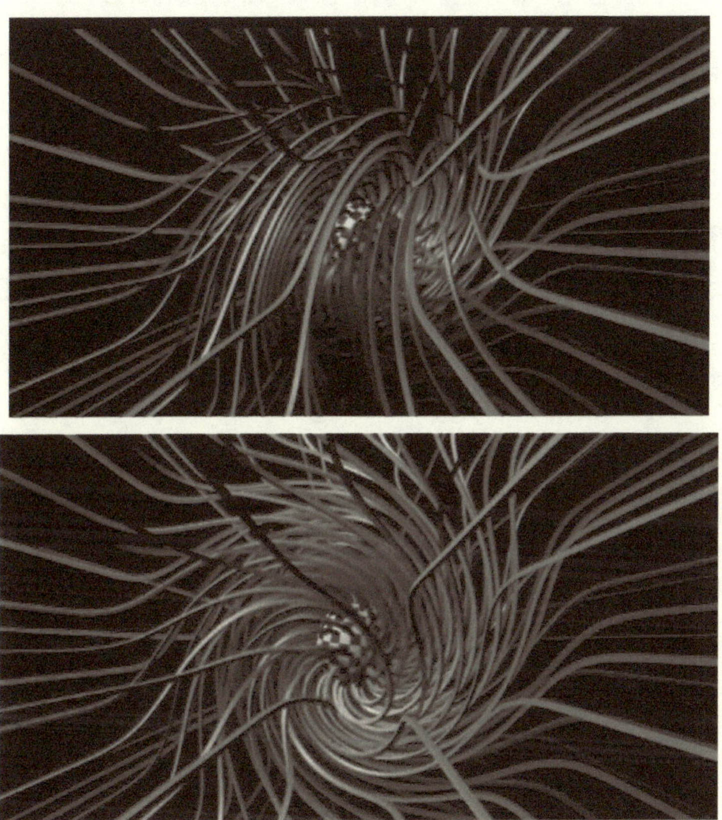

Image 6: Shows a diagrammatic representation of the Spinor model with a central sphere with thread-like connections spiralling around it extending outwards towards infinity. (Image Courtesy: Wikipedia)

A Glimpse of Shiva's Rudraksha

Shiva is often associated with a "Rudraksha," which is spherical and has an irregular surface. The unruly resemblance of the Rudraksha to the spinor model, with pointy-looking NEPs at the surface of a particle, cannot be missed. (see the figure of Spinor)

There is another intriguing resemblance worth noting. Shiva is often depicted wearing ornaments made from Rudraksha beads. A well-known folk story tells of the "Vindhya Mountain and Shiva," which suggests that the entire Universe is encapsulated within a single Rudraksha belonging to Shiva. The multiverse hypothesis posits that there are multiple Universes, each resembling bubbles. It is believed that Shiva has no beginning or end, making him eternal and beyond our Universe. This Universe is merely one of the many that he governs; all Universes can be likened to beads on a "necklace" adorning Shiva's neck or arms.

Determining which of these interpretations holds true is challenging.

Image 7: Shiva's Rudraksha

Image 8: Entire Universe in one frame
(as if it is within a single Rudraksh of Shiva)

Shiva the sculptor, sculpting the whole world or Shiva as an Actor

Vedic description of Shiva as an expert sculptor and an actor is well known.

Shiva, with the help of his countless hands (which represent the snake-like "Push" and "Pull" bands), clings various particles together and sculpts the material world.

Shiva is said to take different roles implying that there is a single universal Deity called "Parabrahma" who takes different forms according to the need. Thus, Vishnu or Bramha are different forms of Shiva itself which perform different functions and are equivalent to Shiva. The names are just a figment of our mind and can be twisted. In other words, one can very well say that Shiva and Bramha are different forms of Vishnu etc.

In verse 1 of Rudr Ashtakam given below, Shiva is विभुं i.e. all-capable, व्यापकं i.e. all encompassing, ब्रम्ह i.e. Shiva is Bramhan himself, वेदस्वरूपम् i.e. embodiment of the Vedas i.e. knowledge itself. Further it says that Shiva is निजं I.e. fully absorbed within self, निर्गुणं i.e. beyond the three gunas, निर्विकल्पं i.e. is changeless and निरीहं i.e. does not move.

नमामीशमीशान निर्वाणरूपं

विभुं व्यापकं ब्रह्मवेदस्वरूपम् ।

निजं निर्गुणं निर्विकल्पं निरीहं

चिदाकाशमाकाशवासं भजेऽहम् ॥१॥

namāmi-shamishān-nirvāan-roopaṁ

vibhuṁ -vyāpakaṁ -brahma-veda-swarupaṁ

nijaṁ -nirgunaṁ -nirvikalpaṁ -nirihaṁ

chidākāshaṁ -ākasa-vāsaṁ -bhaje-[a]haṁ ||1||

I offer my reverence to Bhagavan Ishaan (Shiva),

whose essence symbolizes freedom, who is omnipotent,

who pervades all existence, who is the Parabrahma Paramatma,

and who embodies the Vedas

He is ever immersed in the pure self, transcending all qualities (sattva, rajas, tamas),

unchanging and unmoving,

and vast and all-encompassing like the sky.

I venerate that divine Bhagavan Shiva ||1||

The All-encompassing “field of nothingness” is changeless and does not move but is the force behind all that changes. The field of nothingness represents the Universal unchanging background co-ordinate system in DGR.

Shiva is Gangadhar

Shiva embodies the concept of destruction. In the context of DGR, photons which are packets of positive energy, have destruction occurring within them.

Shiva is referred to as “Gangadhar” because he holds the river Ganga in his matted hair. (See the verse 3 third line of Rudr Ashtakam given below)

स्फुरन्मौलिकल्लोलिनी चारुगङ्गा

लसद्भालबालेन्दु कण्ठे भुजङ्गा ॥३॥

sphuran-mauli-kallolini-chāru-gangā

lasad- bhālbalendu -kanthe-bhujangā ||3||

From whose matted hair flows the sacred Ganga, whose head is adorned with a crescent moon,

and whose neck is gracefully beautified by a garland of serpents. ||3||

The Ganga symbolizes all rivers, representing the water drawn from the ocean.

During storms and heavy rainfall, I often notice a massive amount of water cascading from the sky to the Earth. Just moments ago, this colossal volume of water, which nearly flooded the entire street, was suspended in the atmosphere. It made me wonder: Who or what possesses the strength to hold such vast amounts of water? The answer lies in the Sun's energy, which elevates water from the ocean and makes it accessible to nature. The particles of light, or photons, represent tiny packets where destruction occurs.

Shiva is Neelkanth and Bholenath

Shiva is also called "Neelkanth" (See the 4th verse, second line of Rudr Ashtakam) as he drank the "Halahal" poison that came out of the process of "Samudra Manthan" or churning of the great ocean of milk (discussed separately). He is also often called Bholenath. He is said to have no "Ahankar" i.e. he has no need for importance for himself. He is self-less, kind, compassionate (दयालम् – verse 4 of Rudr Ashtakam). He removes detachment from worldly things – renunciation (कलातीत - who is beyond worldly materials).

चलत्कुण्डलं भ्रूसुनेत्रं विशालं

प्रसन्नाननं नीलकण्ठं दयालम् ।

मृगाधीशचर्माम्बरं मुण्डमालं

प्रियं शङ्करं सर्वनाथं भजामि ॥४॥

chalat-kundalaṁ -bhru-sunetraṁ -vishālaṁ

prasannā-nannaṁ -neel-khantaṁ -dayālaṁ

mrigā-dhisha-charmāṁ -baraṁ -munda-mālaṁ

priyaṁ -shankaraṁ -sarva-nathaṁ -bhajāmi ||4||

(I offer my salutations to Bhagavan Shiva),

whose earrings sway gracefully as he moves,

whose eyebrows and eyes are strikingly beautiful and expansive, whose face radiates bliss,

who has a blue-hued throat and is filled with compassion.

He is adorned in garments made from tiger skin and wears a garland of skulls.

I revere the beloved Shankar, the supreme lord of all. ||4||

He is always benevolent or altruistic (कल्याण कारी) and who is capable of ending the cycle of creation (कल्पान्तकारी – verse 6 Rudr Ashtakam).

कलातीतकल्याण कल्पान्तकारी

सदा सज्जनानन्ददाता पुरारी ।

चिदानन्दसंदोह मोहापहारी

प्रसीद प्रभो मन्मथारी ॥६॥

kalātīta-kalyān-kalpānta-kāri

sada-sajjan-[ā]nanda-dāta-purāri

chidānanda-sandoha-moha-pahāri

prasida-prasida-prabho-manmathāri||6||

(I offer my salutations to Bhagavan Shiva),

who transcends material existence, who strives for the upliftment of others,

who brings an end to the cycle of creation, who grants joy to the virtuous (dharmic individuals),

and who vanquished the demon Tripurasuras (representing adharmic forces),

who eradicates attachments and imparts wisdom to his devotees.

O compassionate one, O compassionate one, destroyer of Kamadeva, please be gracious. ||6||

The PEP core where Shiva is supposed to suck everything to itself and has no tendency to repel. It would attract even the NEPs. NEP's where Brahma is supposed to reside, who on the contrary would be full of ahankara (tendency to repel) and would think only about "me" and due to this, would repel everything away. This goes well with the fact that NEPs cannot form aggregates and thus can't attain a significant size or importance by themselves.

The God particle

The Higgs boson, the particle predicted by physics, giving rise to the mass of every particle, is equivalent to the concentric spherical PC aggregates moving inwards with alternating development of PC vacuum just within the spheres. The Higgs boson is also called the God particle.

The Higgs field condenses around a particle with more mass while it fails to condense around a particle with less or no mass. This matches pretty closely to the description of this field of nothingness in DGR wherein the field of nothingness causes the surrounding PCs to move rapidly (faster than the speed of light) around the more massive particle while this compensatory inward movement of PCs is much less rapid since the rate and amount of destruction per unit "Universal time" is much less around a particle with less mass or massless particle respectively.

Shiva is Chandrashekhar

If we apply similar logic, Shiva, the force behind the incessant destruction happening at the centre of every particle that constitutes the Earth, is the primary reason for the Gravity of the Earth that holds the moon in its place. (Verse 3 last line says Shiva holds the crescent Moon on his forehead)

स्फुरन्मौलिकल्लोलिनी चारुगङ्गा

लसद्भालबालेन्दु कण्ठे भुजङ्गा ॥३॥

sphuran-mauli-kallolini-chāru-gangā

lasad- bhālbalendu -kanthe-bhujangā ||3||

From whose matted hair flows the sacred Ganga, whose head is adorned with a crescent moon,

and whose neck is gracefully beautified by a garland of serpents. ||3||

Shiva is the one with no beginning and no end (Anaadi Anant)

Rudr Ashtakam describes Shiva as beyond knowledge, speech and senses (गिराज्ञानगोतीतमीशं) *i.e.* he cannot be described in words or speech, he cannot be understood by knowledge or felt/seen/heard/tasted by senses.

निराकारमोङ्कारमूलं तुरीयं

गिराज्ञानगोतीतमीशं गिरीशम् ।

nirākar-omkār-mulaṁ -turiyaṁ

girā-gyāan-gotī-tamīsaṁ -girīśaṁ

(I offer my salutations to Bhagavan Shiva),

who is without form, who embodies the essence of Omkara,

the fundamental source of creation,

who resides in the transcendent state where Brahman is realized,

who is beyond words, thought, and sensory perception,

who reigns over Kailash

There is no way to characterize or even predict how the Nothingness that pervades the whole Universe or that lies beyond the edge of the Universe, that we inhabit, will be. Does it have any boundaries? How many other Universes can be there within this nothingness? There is no answer to this question in DGR. However, the Vedas say that countless Universes like these exist beyond the Universe we live in. The Hindu philosophy aligns well with the concept of the Multiverse.

The verse 4 of Rudr Ashtakam declares that Shiva is प्रचण्डं i.e. enormous in size, प्रकृष्टं i.e. superior to all, प्रगल्भं i.e. eternal unborn and परेशं i.e. all powerful (deity/parameshwara). It further says that Shiva is अखण्डं i.e. fully complete all by himself, अजं i.e. has no birth, भानुकोटिप्रकाशं i.e. has the effulgence of a million suns.

प्रचण्डं प्रकृष्टं प्रगल्भं परेशं

अखण्डं अजं भानुकोटिप्रकाशं ।

prachandaṁ -prakristaṁ -pragalbhaṁ -pareshaṁ

akhandaṁ -ajaṁ -bhānu-koti-prakāshaṁ

(I offer my salutations to Bhagavan Shiva),

who is immense, supreme, valiant, and the ultimate Parmeshwar, who is whole, everlasting, and whose brilliance rivals that of a million suns.

The Universe has many large stars and supermassive black holes which according to DGR has massive energy in the form of destruction happening within. Shiva is all that destruction put together. The source of energy for all of them is Shiva. Shiva is bigger/greater than all of them put together.

There was a start for this Universe. The cycles of Creation and Destruction of the Bramha go on in succession with the formation and destruction of Universes. But Shiva has no beginning or end. The sixth verse of Rudr Ashtakam says that Shiva is कल्पान्तकारी i.e. the one who ends a कल्प or Kalp i.e. a single cycle of creation and destruction of the Universe. (See the section on Shiva is Bholenath)

If the soul is a small drop of Shiva or Parabrahma, then the Bhagavad Gita says the following

---

Bhagavad Gita: Chapter 2, Verse 20

न जायते म्रियते वा कदाचि

नायं भूत्वा भविता वा न भूयः |

अजो नित्यः शाश्वतोऽयं पुराणो

न हन्यते हन्यमाने शरीरे || 20||

na jāyate mriyate vā kadāchin

nāyaṁ bhūtvā bhavitā vā na bhūyaḥ

ajo nityaḥ śhāśhvato 'yaṁ purāṇo

na hanyate hanyamāne śharīre

The soul is neither born, nor does it ever die; nor having once existed, does it ever cease to be. The soul is without birth, eternal, immortal, and ageless. It is not destroyed when the body is destroyed.

(Courtesy: https://www.holy-bhagavad-gita.org)

A Glimpse of Shiva's Damru

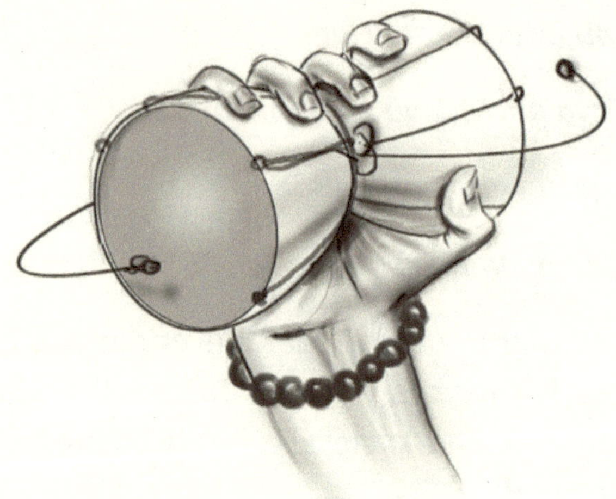

Figure: Shiva's Damru

Shiva has a ***"Damru"*** in his hand and is often called the Kaal or Mahakaal or Time. A damru is a small hourglass-shaped drum-like instrument with strands with beads attached to one end while the other end is attached to the hourglass. A rotatory rocking movement of a Damru causes the beads at the end of the strands to strike the surface of the drums, thus making a sound. A rhythmical rocking creates a repetitive sound from the damru called ***"naad".***

Shiva is the ***time-keeper*** of the Universe (Shrishti) and the entire Universe is said to run at the rhythm or the "naad" of Shiva's damru.

The alternating pole shifting of the two poles of the model of the charged particle in DGR, wherein the outer NEPs forming the surface of the lattice keep pushing each other away from the "pole of excessive NEPs" and move towards the "pole of a void in NEPs", thus explaining the spin of the charged particle is noticeably similar to the strands of a Damru. The Push-Pull bands emanating from the surface diverging out as a spiral towards the infinity outwards explain the spin ½ of the charged particle well. The Push-Pull bands reverberate alternatingly shifting the location of formation and the direction of propagation of the push-pull bands.

The pulsatile dance of alternating waves generated out of this pole-shifting movement of the NEPs caused due to the central pull force of Shiva's destruction is the reason for the Electromagnetic waves emitted by a charged particle, with the Push-Pull bands being the electric (and magnetic) flux.

These NEPs or Negative energy particles are regions where constant "Creation of PCs" is happening. So, the Space is expanding and the newly created PCs are pushed out in all directions as compensation around each NEP. They have a tendency to push each other away and push the "Positive-energy centre" away as well.

Thus, they cannot fall further inside. The compensatory changes in the surrounding space would lead to the formation of narrow corridors of actively expanding space to compensate for the active creation within NEPs, narrow corridors of contracting space to compensate for the destruction caused by the PEP aggregation at the centre and narrow corridors of relatively less actively contracting space in between them.

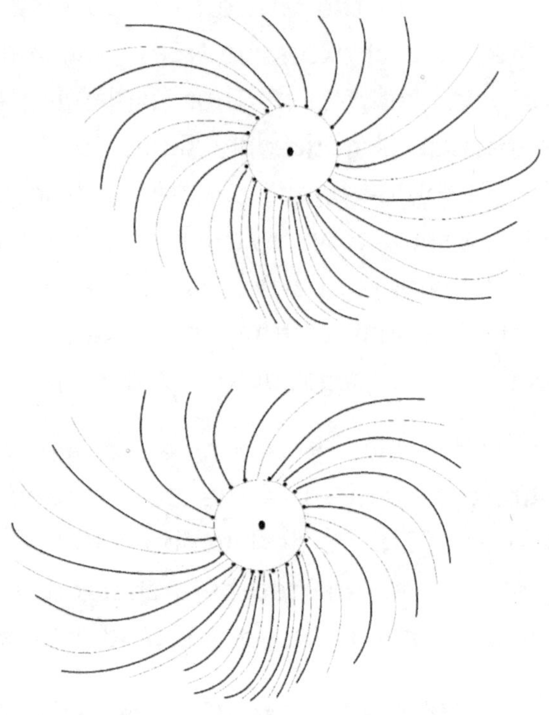

Figure: Shows how the pull bands (here shown as lighter lines) emanating from the gaps between NEPs and Push bands (shown here as darker lines) emanating from the location of NEPs in the lattice move outwards in a spiral manner. The Poles keep alternating so that the NEP excess pole is up momentarily and down momentarily. This creates an alternating rotatory movement of the Push Pull bands which would look very similar to Damru. Note that the centre is where the PEP aggregate core exists and an extreme amount of Destruction

of PCs is happening here while the small dots on the outer circle is where NEPs exist and Creation is happening here

These narrow corridors are akin to the snakes (wrapped around the neck of the PEP aggregate which represents Shiva) or threads with attached beads.

The expanding bands are called Push bands and contracting bands are called Pull bands. These bands spiral outwards at supra-luminal speeds out from the spherical NEP lattice. The model resembles a spinor here. (see the figure of Spinor). These bands can help us explain many concepts in modern physics like the "spin of a charged particle" and electromagnetic or other bonds or forces of Nature.

As shown in the figure, the constant shifting of the location of the NEPs away from the "Excessive NEP pole" to the "NEP Deficient pole" changes the polarity of the particle and explains the phenomenon known as the "Superposition of spin" of a charged particle.

A Glimpse of Shiva's dance - Tandav

Shiva is often depicted as Nataraja wherein Shiva is shown dancing and crushing a demon (named Apasmara Purusha – indicating ignorance) under his feet while flames move out from all directions. The form of Shiva's dance is called Tandav Nritya.

The Large Hadron Collider in CERN also has a large statue of Nataraja just outside its office in Geneva, Switzerland.

Figure: A statue of Nataraja

The reason why LHC has a statue of Shiva is not clear although some say that the Tandav Nritya of Shiva is often associated with how the Electron moves within the atom.

In DGR, the push-pull bands emanating away from the charged particle move outwards with supra-luminal velocities and interact with the other charged particles. The theory can successfully explain the phenomenology of Quantum Chromodynamics within the nucleus as well. However, it is difficult to include all that in detail here.

The Push-Pull bands emanating from the Electrons outside the nucleus can interact with similar bands within the nucleus. These interactions have to happen faster than the speed of light since the speed of light is too slow. This doesn't violate Relativity as what is travelling faster than the speed of light is expanding or contracting space.

The Electron would then move its position every 3-4 Planck times. This is extremely fast. Note that electron being a particle with mass (unlike the push-pull bands which are just regions of space) cannot travel faster than the speed of light i.e. faster than 1 Planck length in 1 Planck time.

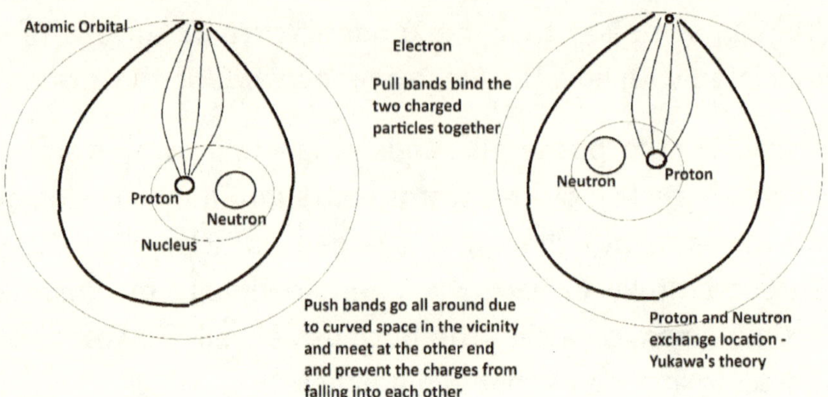

Figure: Shows a diagrammatic representation of how Pull bands pull the two interacting charged particles bonded together in an atom while the Push bands that go around the nucleus keep the particles from coming too close. The location of proton within the nucleus keeps changing and so does the location of the Electron. Note that the process is more complicated than depicted since Protons and Neutrons are made of Quarks and the Push Pull bands are essentially like waves of reverberating Space time and not just lines as shown. Note that only few Push pull bands are shown for clarity. The bands will always be alternating in location and reverberating in dimension. The Push band shown all around the nucleus moves out like a cone and on curving around the nucleus completes a shape similar to a 3-dimensional drop of water.

Yukawa's theory suggests that the positions of protons within the nucleus are not fixed; they constantly change. The neighbouring neutrons absorb small particles known as pi mesons. When a neutron absorbs a pi meson, it is converted into a proton, while the proton that loses the pi meson becomes a neutron.

This also explains the wave-particle duality of the electron and quantization of angular momentum i.e. it explains why the Electron is allowed to stay only in certain orbits or orbitals and can form standing waves. This is because, only at this distance from the central core, a standing wave of the Push band forms and provides the repulsive force that can counteract the attractive force between the coinciding pull bands of the interacting charges within the atom. Note that the Push band curves around the PEP core as space here is curved just like the space just outside a Blackhole where light can travel in circles and forms the accretion disk around the Blackhole and makes it glow. The PEP aggregate is thus akin to a Black hole at the centre, gobbling up space rapidly and probably also has an event horizon within which the PCs move inwards faster than the speed of light.

Again, explaining this in detail is beyond the purview of this book. However detailed analysis can give potential clues to why more complex atoms have different orbitals of varying shapes.

Shiva's Trishul

The primary weapon of Shiva is the trident also called the Trishul.

In Rudr Ashtakam verse 5, Shiva is being called as शूलपाणिं which means the one who holds a trident in his hand.

त्र्यःशूलनिर्मूलनं शूलपाणिं

भजेऽहं भवानीपतिं भावगम्यम् ॥५॥

trayah-shula-nirmulanaṁ -shula-pāniṁ

bhaje-[a]haṁ -bhavāni-patim-bhāva-gamyaṁ ||5||

Who wields a trident in his hand and removes all sorrows,

guiding devotees beyond the three gunas.

I revere the consort of Bhavani, who can be realized through devotion. ||5||

Opinions vary regarding the significance of the trident. But if we consider Shiva as the Parabrahma i.e. the supreme universal deity equivalent to both Bramha and Vishnu, then Shiva itself is responsible for the three processes of Destruction, Creation and Compensation. Effectively, Shiva or Parabrahma has these three Gunas under control. The trident may be a metaphorical representation of the three Gunas and how they are utilized by him to be in control.

Shiva's formless form (Nirgun)

Shiva or the Parabrahma is supposed to have two forms Sagun (with form) and Nirgun (formless).

The third line of the first verse of Rudr Ashtakam given before also says the same.

निजं निर्गुणं निर्विकल्पं निरीहं

चिदाकाशमाकाशवासं भजेऽहम् ॥१॥

nijaṁ -nirgunaṁ -nirvikalpaṁ -nirihaṁ

chidākāshaṁ -ākasa-vāsaṁ -bhaje-[a]haṁ ||1||

He is ever immersed in the pure self, transcending all qualities (sattva, rajas, tamas),

unchanging and unmoving,

and vast and all-encompassing like the sky.

I venerate that divine Bhagavan Shiva ||1||

If we consider PC vacuum in between the PCs as an omnipresent field that can derive information from the system about whereabouts of particles and is conscious and intelligent at the same time, to enter into the complex soup of "Panchamahabhootas" (as discussed elsewhere in the section of union of Shiva with Shakti) that can actively bring about changes within the cell to make it alive, it can be considered as the Formless form of Shiva or Nirgun form. Nirgun can also be interpreted as beyond the three gunas i.e. unaffected by the effect of the three gunas.

Shiva is present in every particle

There are many verses in the Vedic literature which suggest that Shiva is present in every particle (kan kan mein - कण कण में)

It doesn't take too much ingeniousness to realise this co-incidence. Every particle has active destruction happening at its Positive Energy Particle core as per DGR. This goes well with Shiva being present at the core of every particle.

Shiva is Mahakaal or the ultimate time keeper

Time is a complex concept that has proven difficult to understand. Before the advent of Einstein's Special Relativity (SR), scientists believed that time was absolute and uniform at all locations. Many in the pre-Einsteinian era thought they had a solid grasp on the nature of time.

However, with Einstein's Special Relativity, it became clear that time is not as straightforward as previously thought. It was established that a moving observer would perceive the speed of light as constant in a vacuum, meaning that time runs differently for observers in motion compared to those at rest. This concept points out that time passes more quickly for a stationary observer than for someone in motion.

With the introduction of General Relativity, it was further revealed that time also slows down in the vicinity of a gravitationally active body, a phenomenon known as gravitational time dilation. This led to the understanding of time as an entity closely linked to space, and the term "spacetime" was coined.

Today, with the emergence of Loop Quantum Gravity—a proposed theory of gravity—time appears to vanish altogether. In quantum mechanics and the standard model, time is treated as a static background entity, disconnected from the fabric of space.

One of the unsolved mysteries in physics is the arrow of time, which refers to the observed one-directional flow of time. No one has conclusively explained why time only seems to move forward, despite a concept known as time-reversal symmetry, which suggests that the laws of physics would remain consistent even if time flowed in the opposite direction.

In his theories, Einstein introduced a term called T_0, which represents the time experienced by an observer located at an infinite distance from all gravitationally active bodies. For this hypothetical observer, there would be no effects of gravitational time dilation.

The location of this observer would indeed be outside the Universe.

Vedas propound that Shiva is the Maha kaal or the deity of time. This means that Shiva is time itself or Shiva is the controller of time. It is said that everything moves forward with the rhythm of Shiva's Damru.

The 2nd verse of Rudr Ashtakam exclaims that Shiva is महाकालकालं *i.e. Shiva is superior to time or is the Lord of Time.*

करालं महाकालकालं कृपालं

गुणागारसंसारपारं नतोऽहम् ॥२॥

karālaṁ -mahakāl-kālaṁ -kripālaṁ

gunā-gāara-sansār-pāraṁ -na-to-[a]haṁ ||2||

who surpasses both Vikral and Mahakal,

who is merciful,

and who guides devotees beyond the worldly existence rooted in the qualities of nature.

I revere that divine Bhagavan Shiva. ||2||

In DGR, this Universe has an edge beyond which there is nothingness. The edge of the Universe has PC vacuum just outside it. Thus, the PCs keep moving outwards with constant Compensation by active Creation from within. This constant outward movement of the Universe gives the direction to the arrow of time. Every moment, there is a new form of the Universe. The Universe is all changing, i.e. the location of particles within it keeps changing. Every subsequent moment of time creates a different state of the Universe. The past becomes history and future has never happened yet. This, although extremely logical, contradicts significantly with the presently accepted forms of Special Relativity and General Relativity which steer towards an entity called as "block time" wherein all past present and future are happening/exist all at once.

Our theory would say that there are two different versions of "time". The constantly moving forward entity of time is the Universal time. This Universal time is the Time of Shiva and can be measured only when you go out of the Universe. The constantly varying status of space, actively expanding at some places while actively contracting at other places makes the detection of this "real" time or Universal time, almost impossible. The only time we can measure is local time, which varies depending on the expansion or contraction of space. While this might seem to contradict special relativity at first glance, it can effectively explain our experimental findings and observations.

Our theory suggests that both time and space are not infinitely divisible. The smallest possible "atom-equivalent" of the fabric of space is a Planck Compartment measuring 1 Planck length. However, a Planck Compartment can move at significantly smaller distances per Planck time. So, the smallest possible length cannot be Planck length. Similarly, the lag between one PC movement and the next outer PC movement cannot be 1 PT as this would be too slow and this would put a significant limit to how fast space can expand or contract. Thus, the smallest possible measure of time is not 1 Planck time but could be several orders of magnitude or even several hundred orders of magnitude smaller. This can actually be measured or calculated if we are able to measure the speed of Entanglement which indicates how fast the two entangled particles can communicate.

The rate at which PCs are destroyed at the PEP core determines the pole shift in DGR. This pole shift creates the term superposition of spin of the charged particle wherein the spin keeps changing from one direction to the other. These movements happen so fast (i.e. within a few Planck times) that to us with a limited ability to comprehend these miniature values of time, it appears that the spin is in superposition – i.e. the electron is with both right-handed and left-handed spin at the same time. This is like us not able to see the blades of a fast-moving fan.

These movements look like the rhythmic movement of strings of a Damru. The rate of this rhythmic movement of the push-pull bands spiralling outwards is possibly unaffected by the status of Spatial contraction outside and thus is a good potential means of measuring Universal time.

Indeed, the Observer at an infinite distance from all gravitationally active bodies, whose time was called T_0 by Einstein oddly fits well with Shiva.

Thus, it makes good sense that Shiva is called Kaal or Mahakaal.

If this was confusing, more confusion is yet to come with the time of Bramha.

Parabrahma

Who is superior or the three Trideva? – a folk tale

There is a story in the Puranas about the **Trideva**.

This was a time when nothing had yet been formed. Only *Shunya* (the void, or zero) existed.

Then, Lord Vishnu was created, and from his umbilicus, a lotus emerged. From this lotus, Lord Brahma was born.

Soon after, a debate erupted between the two of them about who was greater or more important. At that moment, a large lingam—a cylindrical pillar of fire—appeared in front of them, and a voice came from within. The voice declared that whoever could find the ends of this fiery pillar would be considered superior.

Lord Vishnu ascended toward the sky in search of the upper end, while Lord Brahma descended toward *Pataal Lok* (the underworld i.e. the miniature world, where the Asuras would later reside). After a long and fruitless search, neither of them could find the end. However, Lord Brahma encountered a Ketaki flower and proclaimed that it would serve as evidence of his journey to the lower end of the pillar.

At that moment, a voice from the pillar spoke, declaring: "This is not the truth." Lord Shiva then appeared before them and explained that all three of them—Vishnu, Brahma, and Shiva—were one and the same, and that Vishnu and Brahma had been born from Shiva, from this very lingam.

Shiva then cursed Lord Brahma for speaking a lie, stating: "Because of your *ahankara* (ego, or self-importance), no one will ever worship you."

It is impossible to ascertain the literal truth of this Puranic story as there is a possibility of it being dramatized a bit to make people with poor knowledge (agyan) understand these difficult concepts.

However, it raises an intriguing question: In a time when nothing had been formed—when no elements, materials, or particles existed—how did the Ketaki flower come into being? Perhaps the flower is meant to be understood metaphorically. The Ketaki flower, with its small, overlapping petals, could represent the lotus or a lattice structure, similar to the lattice made by **NEPs** (Negative Energy Particles) described in text elsewhere.

Shiva and Vishnu are the same

If the compensation process is due to the "nothingness field" then compensation is due to Shiva, i.e. Shiva is equivalent to Vishnu. This is essentially the term Brahman or Parabrahma (परब्रम्ह).

Hanuman (an avatar of Shiva) is said to have Ram (who is the avatar of Vishnu) within his heart. Thus, Vishnu is within the heart of Shiva. This is another way of saying that this Universe is within A huge zone of Nothingness or is within a Black hole.

Parabrahma (परब्रम्ह) is omnipresent and is responsible for everything that moves

ईशा वास्यमिदं सर्वं यत्किञ्च जगत्यां जगत्।

तेन त्यक्तेन भुञ्जीथा मा गृधः कस्यस्विद्धनम् ॥

Ishā vāsyam idaṁ sarvaṁ yatkinch jagtyām jagat

Ten tyakten bhunjithā mā grudh-ha kasyasvid-dhanaṁ

"All that exists in the universe, both animate and inanimate, is pervaded by the Supreme Lord. Therefore, you should enjoy the resources with detachment, taking only what is necessary, without attachment, and never hoard as though they belong to you."

The Isha Upanishad given above says that in this everchanging (ephemeral) Universe, "Ish" i.e. the Parabrahma is present everywhere and is the primary reason or force behind every change. So, everything that we can see and everything that we own belongs to the lord. And we should renounce or avoid lusting on, trying to steal or enjoy someone else's possessions i.e. considering what we don't own as ours. This verse teaches us to give up attachment to worldly things i.e. significance of renunciation.

In DGR, the first part makes complete sense. There is nothing in the name and one can change the name, from Parabrahma to something else, if one wishes to. However, it's plausible that a single "entity" could be in control of all three processes. The theory doesn't make any predictions or define limitations for the underlying theory that supports its assumptions. Nevertheless, an intelligent, aware entity capable of managing the three processes known as Parabrahma (परब्रम्ह) is certainly a possibility that cannot be dismissed.

Brahman is real and the world is an appearance and is unreal

ब्रह्म सत्यं जगन्मिथ्या जीवो ब्रह्मैव नापरः।

अनेन वेद्यं सच्छास्त्रमिति वेदान्तडिण्डिमः॥

(Courtesy: sanskritforus.com)

bramha satyaṁ jagatmithyā jivo bramhaiva nāparah

anen vedyaṁ sacchastramiti vedāntadindimah

Meaning:

Brahman, the ultimate reality, is the only truth (it cannot be categorized as either real or unreal). Everything else, including the material world, is illusory or false (mithya). The individual self (jiva) is not separate from Brahman. The apparent distinction between the individual and the universal is an illusion created by ignorance (avidya). This must be recognized as the authentic scripture, as affirmed by the teachings of Vedanta. The verse explains that the external world, with all its diversity, is not the ultimate reality. Instead, Brahman is the singular truth that pervades all.

This is one of the commonest taught verses from the Vedanta which is highly confusing and often thought to be controversial or ill-understood. This whole World or this Universe is pretty evident to us. The verse is telling us that whatever World we can see is full of Maya i.e. deception. Some say that the verse indicates the material world is destructible i.e. Vinashi compared to the Brahman or Parabrahma which is "Avinashi" i.e. cannot be destroyed. Although often quoted, these explanations are not convincing.

A common explanation provided by Vedanta teachers is the example of "the rope and the snake." In this analogy, the rope represents reality, while our misperception of it as a snake is considered unreal. This misperception arises from Maya, which refers to deception or flaws in perception created by our minds. Although this analogy is simple to grasp, some may find it insufficiently convincing.

Questions that remain are,

- I am in my house, sitting on the chair, sitting in front of the laptop. Is any of this real?
- Is this Earth Real?
- Are the Eight Billion people living on it real?
- Are the 10^{80} particles in this Universe real then?
- Are the laws of physics real then?

The verse is trying to say that all these do exist but they appear to us as they do due to Maya or our mind's deception. All of them are nothing but Brahman (ब्रह्म).

If we analyse this verse with context to our theory, everything starts making sense.

If we dig deeper, we find that everything can be understood through three fundamental processes: the destruction of Planck Compartments (PCs), the creation of PCs, and the shifting or compensatory processes occurring elsewhere. Ultimately, all of this is nothing but Brahman or Parabrahma (परब्रम्ह). This means that at the core, only Brahman truly exists. The material world we perceive is limited by what our sense organs can interpret. A significant extent of the Universe that exists is beyond our sensory perception. Therefore, the world is essentially an illusion or an appearance.

Salutations to all gods ultimately goes to a single deity

Vaishanava Purana asserts that salutations to any form of God ultimately go to Keshav which is another name from Shri Hari Vishnu.

आकाशात् पतितं तोयं यथा गच्छति सागरम् ।

सर्वदेवनमस्कारं केशवं प्रतिगच्छति ॥

ākāśāt patitaṃ toyaṃ yathā gacchati sāgaram /

sarvadevanamaskāraṃ keśavaṃ pratigacchati //

Meaning:

As the water that falls down in rain from anywhere in the sky finally reaches the Ocean, the worship of any divine aspect ultimately reaches the Supreme Being.

Skandha Purana gives a similar assertion that salutations to all gods ultimately reaches Maheshwar which is another name of Shiva.

यथा तोयप्रवाहाणां समुद्रः परमावधि ।

तथैव सर्व मार्गाणां साक्षान्निष्ठा महेश्वरः ।।

yathā toyapravāhanām Samudra paramāvadhi

tathaiva sarv margānam sakshannishtā maheshwarah

Meaning:

As all streams ultimately empty themselves into the ocean,

so all these paths ultimately lead to the Great Lord Himself.

Other Deities like Laxmi, Saraswati, Parvati and Ganesh

A Glimpse of "Samudra Manthan" and birth of Lakshmi, Kamdhenu and other jewels

As discussed earlier, the word "Kshirsagar" or the ocean of milk, where Vishnu resides, can be metaphorically reinterpreted in many different ways. Vedas say that this Universe was created when there was nothing (created within Nothingness or Shunya). This universe was made in a Cosmic Egg called Hiranyagarbha.

The current theories of Physics suggest that there was nothing before the creation event and at the time of creation, the Universe started with a "Big Bang". Although no one can definitively explain what the Big Bang was, we can describe events that occurred shortly after it in great detail. To address the uniformity observed across different regions of the Universe, the "theory of Inflation" was proposed. This inflationary cosmology eliminates the need for faster-than-light communication of information about temperature between distant corners of the Universe.

The Cosmic Microwave Background (CMB) represents the light that has travelled since the Universe began and has now reached us. It reveals extremely minor fluctuations in temperature, raising the question: how did one part of the Universe know the temperature of another distant part?

This issue does not arise in Dynamic General Relativity, which allows for the active expansion of space. In this framework, photons can take a ride on the expanding space, enabling information to be transmitted throughout the Universe without violating the speed limit established by Special Relativity. Special Relativity necessitates that electromagnetic radiation, which carries information about heat, must travel at the speed of light and cannot exceed this speed. Thus, DGR eliminates the need for additional assumption of inflation. In other words, inflation is already present in DGR.

In the early age of the Universe, there were no particles—only radiation. The mixture of all frequencies of photons would have appeared white, resembling an ocean of milk. In this ocean of "metaphorical milk," processes occurred that led to the formation of charged particles. The bonding of these particles gave rise to everything we can see today.

The process of "Hadron" synthesis is explained in detail in Dynamic General Relativity and is not difficult to understand. In this, positive energy tends to come together, while negative energy has an innate tendency to remain separate, thereby coating the positive energy core.

If Positive energy is considered "good" representing the "Devas' and Negative energy is considered "bad" representing the "Asuras", then the Samudra Manthan is nothing but

"Churning" of this cosmic ocean of "metaphorical milk" by these two opposing forces leading to the creation of the charged particles and later electromagnetic bonding. This churning was done by the snake called "Vasuki" which wraps around the neck of Shiva, as per the ancient tales.

The process of Samudra Manthan produced various "ratnas" or jewels, including Devi Laxmi, the consort of Vishnu. Devi Laxmi symbolizes prosperity and embodies everything created through the complex electromagnetic bonding resulting from this churning.

It remains unclear whether this "churning" of the metaphorical ocean of milk, which took place at the beginning of creation in DGR through the interaction of positive and negative energies, is directly related to the story of Samudra Manthan. The narrative told in the Puranas features numerous characters and is quite dramatic. Samudra Manthan was said to be performed in search of "Amrit," the "potion of immortality," and also produced other elements, including a poison known as "Halahal" or "Kalakut," which do not align with our theory.

Additionally, Samudra Manthan is described as a historical event, with no claim that this "Manthan" is either ongoing or happens continuously. In contrast, the "churning of the ocean," driven by positive and negative energies in DGR, occurs continuously within every charged particle and is the fundamental reason behind all bonding, chemistry, and forms. Thus, while remarkable similarities exist, they may not represent the same thing.

Lakshmi, the goddess of prosperity, wealth and beauty - the daughter of Samudra

Devi Laksmi, the consort of Shri Hari Vishnu, represents prosperity wealth and beauty. In the initial period, there were no particles and no bonding. As the metaphorical ocean of milk was churned, electromagnetic bonding ensued, the creation would get converted from a monotonous nothingness of vacuum filled with white radiation to a beautiful array of particles being formed and clumping them together under their gravitational attraction to form beautiful stars and star clusters or galaxies. Thus, it makes sense that the Vedas proclaim that Goddess Laxmi is the daughter of this Kshirsaagar, the milky white ocean made of PCs filled with only radiation. Goddess Laxmi, although associated with wealth (which unfortunately is associated by the ignorant mind with only precious metals and gems and jewels made by these), in reality, is the goddess of the prosperity of different elements with different functions we see in the entire periodic table. Kamdhenu, which is considered an avatar of Devi Lakshmi is the divine mother of all with the form of a cow, and is a symbol of the mother giving everything that the Humans and the animals need to satisfy their hunger.

Saraswati, the Goddess of Knowledge

As the monotonous radiation-filled milky ocean of PCs gets transformed into particles bonding beautifully to produce elements, one more thing would be expected to grow along. The knowledge of which particles bond, how and what the result is, what properties the elements gain and so on. There is no limit to what constitutes "Knowledge" and one cannot define it in a sentence.

Although knowledge plays a key role in the process of creation and evolution, there is no evidence that there is any physical existence to it. The process of formation of charged particles and electromagnetic bonding happens all due to their innate tendency. There is no need for an intelligent creator to modify and carefully select what processes take precedence, as yet.

As more complex elements emerged, the formation of life began, leading to intricate processes within living cells and ultimately resulting in the creation of conscious beings. Consequently, knowledge likely expanded at an exponential rate. In Hinduism, the Goddess Saraswati is associated with this knowledge and is the consort of Brahma.

This may as well be a superficial illusion since this knowledge is an integral part of the Supreme Deity and thus it is the same Parabrahma that is taking different roles as needed.

Saraswati is also considered the Goddess of learning. For this, one has to first understand consciousness as learning is a characteristic of conscious beings. Although there is hope in our theory to branch into a full theory of consciousness, as yet we do not have one.

Parvati or Prakriti

The formation of different elements signifies the beginning of the development of unconscious material things within the Universe. For a long time, most of these elements are expected to be devoid of consciousness. Anything that is material or has a physical existence can be referred to as Prakriti. This includes all the PCs that constitute the Universe and the particles that form and lead to all the PC movements.

There is no universally accepted definition of consciousness. However, generally speaking, consciousness can be described as the ability to actively acquire information from the surroundings, interpret that information, and choose an appropriate line of action from multiple options. In this context, rocks and all particles that interact to form higher-level structures like molecules and crystals are considered unconscious. This unconscious aspect of the universe can be referred to as Prakriti and is described as "Jada," meaning devoid of consciousness.

Even simple elements like iron, gold, and silver are unconscious. But the elements that constitute the biological processes like the plant cells, animal cells, bacteria etc are several orders of magnitude higher in complexity. They are also however unconscious. Thus carbon, oxygen, hydrogen and their various combinations like glucose, water or carbon dioxide are unconscious. The Vedas proclaim that our bodies are made of the five vital elements or "Pancha Mahabhootas" I.e. Apas or jal (water), Agni (fire), Vayu (air), Prithvi (Earth), Aakash (space). All these Pancha-mahabhootas are "Jada" i.e. unconscious. The complex interplay between these leads to the Prakriti which when combined with Shiva the consciousness, forms life.

Shiva and Chit - the Consciousness

As opposed to these "Jada" or non-conscious elements of the Universe, the conscious elements or conscious agents are living beings that possess the ability to derive useful information from their internal milieu and external environment and take appropriate action. A very basic example of this is a cell which can calculate that it has a relative deficiency of "energy" and thus actively chooses to open certain channels to facilitate the absorption of glucose from the surroundings. The purely materialistic scientists might say that this may purely be a chemical interaction, but the fact that the cell chose to act for glucose and not any other molecule like vitamin B or cholesterol means that the cell does have the ability to distinguish between these elements. This ability is lacking in the rocks. Our brain with its functioning is another example of the grave enigma of consciousness. If one is thirsty, one chooses to get up, walk up to the fridge, open the fridge, open the bottle and drink water from it. Each of these activities needs coordinated efforts from multiple muscles of our body. These muscles act purely by chemical physical processes of activation due to the impulses they receive from the brain. However, for this to happen, the specific neurons that supply these muscles must get activated by themselves in the proper order. It is a puzzle how they derive the information of this exact order in which they are supposed to fire unless they derive this information from some external process.

Imagine that you are sitting in a tree house for bird watching and you hear some hissing among the bushes. Then you see with your binoculars and detect a Tiger approaching. The fact that it is a tiger and it is approaching here is well understood by you. However, the unconscious rock just beside the tree has no way of deriving this information. However, there are limitations to this consciousness. You are aware of certain aspects of your environment, but not all. You may recognize there is a tiger, yet you might overlook the ant crawling on the trunk or the spider spinning its web on the neighbouring branch.

This raises an intriguing physical question. If our Universe contains approximately 10^{80} particles (a figure estimated by physicist Paul Dirac while proposing his "Large Number Hypothesis"), and each particle occupies a different location, we can ask: does a universal coordinate system exist that would allow a Supreme Being to know the whereabouts of each of these particles? For example, just as we can use binoculars to determine that a tiger is about 200 feet away near a shrub with white flowers, would this universally conscious being know the position of every particle? Furthermore, does this omniscient entity possess the ability to influence or alter these particles?

The Vedas say that the Supreme deity is omniscient and omnipresent. This means, Shiva is present in and around each of these 10^{80} particles and he can derive information about the whereabouts of each of them. So, if the Vedas have to be believed, Shiva knows the locations of all the particles in our universe and the neurons in our brains and can induce changes within them, which the Vedas call impulses or vritti.

There is an ongoing debate among physicists and philosophers about whether the Universe is deterministic or not. In a deterministic universe, everything is predetermined, much like a marble rolling down a marble-run tract; its path is fixed. In such a universe, nothing—and no one, not even supreme beings—can alter its course. All events unfold according to the laws of nature, such as gravity, electromagnetism, and inertia.

Conversely, in a non-deterministic universe, conscious beings can bring about changes that allow the laws to bend. For instance, a conscious agent could actively change the direction of gravity, causing the marble to ascend the ramp instead of descending. Another conscious agent might alter the slope or direction of the marble run, thereby modifying the speed or path of the marble.

The Vedas suggest that the Parabrahma, a supreme deity, possesses the ability to exert control over everything that moves or changes. According to the Vedas, this divine presence resides within all beings and is responsible for initiating changes. Therefore, the Vedas promote the idea of a non-deterministic universe. They assert that within our bodies lies a conscious soul, akin to a drop in the ocean of Universal Consciousness that permeates the Universe. While our capacity to gather information is limited, it stems from the universal deity's ability to process information.

In our theory, we outline a concept of conscious agents. A conscious agent is an entity capable of producing positive or negative energy actively. The soul, regardless of its nature, has the potential to induce spatial expansion or contraction in specific areas of the brain, thereby firing targeted neurons. Additionally, the soul can extract information from these firing neurons in the sensory parts of the brain, allowing us to perceive tastes, such as sugar or salt, and distinguish colours like blue from red. This phenomenon relates to the enigmatic qualia component of consciousness.

Shiva unites with Shakti (Parvati)- the divine union of body made up of the five material elements (Panch Mahabhootas) and the Soul

There is a famous story in Vedic literature wherein everyone awaits the divine union of Shiva with Shakti.

Prakriti and all its contents, especially the Panch Mahabhootas, are devoid of consciousness and Shiva is a universally present "Conscious field" of nothingness which has the ability of being conscious i.e. deriving knowledge from the environment.

The union of Shiva and Shakti symbolizes the connection between the soul and the non-conscious "Panch Mahabhootas," which are blended in a complex manner. Therefore, the marriage of Shiva and Shakti serves as a metaphor for the beginning of living conscious beings.

Even if we were to experimentally analyse all the contents of a cell, mix them in a small sac made of the cell membrane, and seal it, the resulting sac would not become a living cell. This is because it would lack something beyond the material components found in all living beings. Unlike this artificial sac filled with fluid, living cells can process information and actively change their constituent molecules, which likely involves altering proteins and modifying their activity. This ability to "choose" is something an artificially created sac cannot do. The material complexity of a living cell cannot be replicated with current technology, and thus the concept of a "soul" or "Pran" remains speculative.

However, if this soul does exist, we can at least gain a superficial understanding of it through our theory. The nature of "qualia" continues to be a challenging and elusive question.

Note that this is in no way the end of it since several verses (like the one given below) say that Shakti or Parvati is the other half of Shiva as depicted aptly in the "Ardhanarishwara" form of Shiva. Also, several Puranic verses say that Devi Aadi Shakti or Parvati is present in all living beings as consciousness.

या देवी सर्वभूतेषु चेतनेत्यभिधीयते ।

नमस्तस्यै नमस्तस्यै नमस्तस्यै नमो नमः ॥७॥

yā devi sarvabhūteśhu chetanetyābhidhīyate

namastasyai namastasyai namastasyai namo namah

Meaning:

To that Devi Who in All Beings is Reflected as Consciousness, Salutations to Her, Salutations to Her, Salutations to Her, Salutations again and again.

Thus, the above is for superficial understanding and there is a deeper truth that lies within and our ignorance of the same from a scientific point of view should not be overlooked.

(Courtesy: https://greenmesg.org/stotras/durga/ya_devi_sarvabhutesu.php)

Parvati sculpts out Vinayaka, her son

There is a story wherein Devi Parvati, sculpts a small statue and puts life into it to give birth to Vinayaka, her son. Eventually, Vinayaka becomes Ganesha the God with an elephant head and riding on a mouse. Ganesha has a long trunk and is considered the God of Wisdom and remover of obstacles. It is said in Maha Bhagavata Puran that Vinayaka is Vishnu himself.

It is clear that we humans use our intelligence or wisdom when we run into an obstacle. When any of our work gets stuck, the organ we are most likely to use is the Brain. Anatomically, the human brain has a large trunk-like Spinal cord coming out from it and is on a small mouse-like Cerebellum.

Indeed, the birth of Ganesha with an elephant's head (after Shiva slashes Vinayaka's head in the story) could be the metaphorical way of describing the creation of "the Human Brain". Of course, this is taking this metaphorical thinking too far and may or may not be true. This arguably is the most bizarre and the most controversial speculation. Also, it has nothing to do with the theory.

Ganesha is the God of Wisdom and is the One Who Removes Obstacles

Whenever we face an obstacle, what we use is the "divine" aspect of our Human Brain i.e. the Intellect. Thus, Ganesha the God of Wisdom and the remover of obstacles is within us in the form of the Human Brain.

But if this is true, it may be demonstrating the saying "God helps those who help themselves" and that the primary remover of obstacles is our own brain. God has already given us a divine weapon of Intelligence to solve our problems. If we keep making the wrong decisions, no Messiah will come to save us. We have to take the initiative, use our intelligence and take the appropriate steps to solve our problems and obstacles.

Epilogue

Epilogue

To summarize, only two basic assumptions—namely, the existence of Planck-scale *PCs* (at 1 Planck volume size) and the existence of a *PC* vacuum—along with two time-related assumptions (Universal time and Local time) and three key processes (i.e., destruction of *PCs*, creation of *PCs*, and compensation of voids) are needed to comprehensively explain everything from General Relativity and Quantum Mechanics to Chemistry, Electromagnetism, Quantum Chromodynamics, and Astronomy. This framework can account for everything, from the smallest particles to the largest structures, including the Universe itself. It is extremely versatile, and thus, it is unlikely to be entirely incorrect, although it needs significant refinement and research.

It can be extrapolated to include the Vedic theory of "the three gunas" and sculpted into a working theory of consciousness as well.

The mathematics required for this theory surpasses human capabilities, likely necessitating supercomputers to even derive Newton's laws or the mathematics behind General Relativity. This is because volume conservation must be considered down to a scale smaller than a Planck volume, and time intervals smaller than Planck time need to be accounted for. Nevertheless, this theory has the potential to derive String Theory phenomenologically, helping to narrow down the number of Calabi-Yau manifolds and making significant progress in physics. It could also provide answers to many of the enigmatic riddles currently faced by the field. Additionally, it holds the potential to contribute to the development of a theory of Consciousness.

Needless to say, the theory of Dynamic General Relativity has the potential to surpass General Relativity and deserves much more attention. Sanatani Hindus, who are also enthusiasts of physics, should ensure that *The Theory of the Trideva* reaches its full potential

Rudr Ashtakam, with meaning in English

Rudr Ashtakam, composed by Sant Tulsidas, is a group of eight verses written in the glory of lord Shiva. Although not directly a part of the Vedas, it is derived from the knowledge given in Vedas and hence is often memorised and chanted to pray to lord Shiva. It is given here with meaning just as a reference, as many beliefs and teachings about Lord Shiva can be noted within it.

I do not wish to take credit for the below mentioned verses and their meaning and acknowledge that they have been taken almost as it is from elsewhere just for reference. The original source is mentioned as well. I am thankful to websites like "Stotra.in" who provide shlokas like Rudr Ashtakam with meaning completely free of cost and in public domain.

(Courtesy https://stotra.in/translation/en/sri-mahadev/rudrashtakam)

नमामीशमीशान निर्वाणरूपं

विभुं व्यापकं ब्रह्मवेदस्वरूपम् ।

निजं निर्गुणं निर्विकल्पं निरीहं

चिदाकाशमाकाशवासं भजेऽहम् ॥१॥

namāmi-shamishān-nirvāan-roopaṁ

vibhuṁ -vyāpakaṁ -brahma-veda-swarupaṁ

nijaṁ -nirgunaṁ -nirvikalpaṁ -nirihaṁ

chidākāshaṁ -ākasa-vāsaṁ -bhaje-[a]haṁ ||1||

I offer my reverence to Bhagavan Ishaan (Shiva),

whose essence symbolizes freedom, who is omnipotent,

who pervades all existence, who is the Parabrahma Paramatma,

and who embodies the Vedas

He is ever immersed in the pure self, transcending all qualities (sattva, rajas, tamas),

unchanging and unmoving,

and vast and all-encompassing like the sky.

I venerate that divine Bhagavan Shiva ||1||

निराकारमोङ्करमूलं तुरीयं

गिराज्ञानगोतीतमीशं गिरीशम् ।

करालं महाकालकालं कृपालं

गुणागारसंसारपारं नतोऽहम् ॥२॥

nirākar-omkār-mulaṁ -turiyaṁ

girā-gyāan-gotī-tamīsaṁ -girīśaṁ

karālaṁ -mahakāl-kālaṁ -kripālaṁ

gunā-gāara-sansār-pāraṁ -na-to-[a]haṁ ||2||

(I offer my salutations to Bhagavan Shiva),

who is without form, who embodies the essence of Omkara,

the fundamental source of creation,

who resides in the transcendent state where Brahman is realized,

who is beyond words, thought, and sensory perception,

who reigns over Kailash, who surpasses both Vikral and Mahakal,

who is merciful,

and who guides devotees beyond the worldly existence rooted in the qualities of nature.

I revere that divine Bhagavan Shiva ||2||

तुषाराद्रिसंकाशगौरं गभीरं

मनोभूतकोटिप्रभाश्री शरीरम् ।

स्फुरन्मौलिकल्लोलिनी चारुगङ्गा

लसद्भालबालेन्दु कण्ठे भुजङ्गा ॥३॥

tushāar-[a]-adri-sankāash-gauram-gabhiraṁ

mano-bhuta-koti-prabhā-shri-shariraṁ

sphuran-mauli-kallolini-chāru-gangā

lasad- bhālbalendu -kanthe-bhujangā ||3||

I offer my salutations to Bhagavan Shiva),

who appears resplendent with a bright, snow-like radiance,

who possesses a serene demeanour and whose brilliance

surpasses that of a thousand Kamadeva combined.

From whose matted hair flows the sacred Ganga, whose head is adorned with a crescent moon,

and whose neck is gracefully beautified by a garland of serpents. ||3||

चलत्कुण्डलं भ्रूसुनेत्रं विशालं

प्रसन्नाननं नीलकण्ठं दयालम् ।

मृगाधीशचर्माम्बरं मुण्डमालं

प्रियं शङ्करं सर्वनाथं भजामि ॥४॥

chalat-kundalaṁ -bhru-sunetraṁ -vishālaṁ

prasannā-nannaṁ -neel-khantaṁ -dayālaṁ

mrigā-dhisha-charmāṁ -baraṁ -munda-mālaṁ

priyaṁ -shankaraṁ -sarva-nathaṁ -bhajāmi ||4||

(I offer my salutations to Bhagavan Shiva),

whose earrings sway gracefully as he moves,

whose eyebrows and eyes are strikingly beautiful and expansive, whose face radiates bliss,

who has a blue-hued throat and is filled with compassion.

He is adorned in garments made from tiger skin and wears a garland of skulls.

I revere the beloved Shankar, the supreme lord of all. ||4||

प्रचण्डं प्रकृष्टं प्रगल्भं परेशं

अखण्डं अजं भानुकोटिप्रकाशं ।

त्र्यःशूलनिर्मूलनं शूलपाणिं

भजेऽहं भवानीपतिं भावगम्यम् ॥५॥

prachandaṁ -prakristaṁ -pragalbhaṁ -pareshaṁ

akhandaṁ -ajaṁ -bhānu-koti-prakāshaṁ

trayah-shula-nirmulanaṁ -shula-pāniṁ

bhaje-[a]haṁ -bhavāni-patim-bhāva-gamyaṁ ||5||

(I offer my salutations to Bhagavan Shiva),

who is immense, supreme, valiant, and the ultimate Parmeshwar,

who is whole, everlasting, and whose brilliance rivals that of a million suns.

Who wields a trident in his hand and removes all sorrows,

guiding devotees beyond the three gunas.

I revere the consort of Bhavani, who can be realized through devotion. ||5||

कलातीतकल्याण कल्पान्तकारी

सदा सज्जनानन्ददाता पुरारी ।

चिदानन्दसंदोह मोहापहारी

प्रसीद प्रसीद प्रभो मन्मथारी ॥६॥

kalātīta-kalyān-kalpānta-kāri

sada-sajjan-[ā]nanda-dāta-purāri

chidānanda-sandoha-moha-pahāri

prasida-prasida-prabho-manmathāri||6||

(I offer my salutations to Bhagavan Shiva),

who transcends material existence, who strives for the upliftment of others,

who brings an end to the cycle of creation, who grants joy to the virtuous (dharmic individuals),

and who vanquished the demon Tripurasura (representing adharmic forces),

who eradicates attachments and imparts wisdom to his devotees.

O compassionate one, O compassionate one, destroyer of Kamadeva, please be gracious. ||6||

न यावद् उमानाथपादारविन्दं

भजन्तीह लोके परे वा नराणाम् ।

न तावत्सुखं शान्ति सन्तापनाशं

प्रसीद प्रभो सर्वभूताधिवासं ॥७॥

na-yāvad-umānaath-pādarvindam

bhajantiha-loke-pare-vā-narā-nām

na-tāvat-sukham-shānti-santāap-nāsham

prasida-prabho-sarva-bhutā-dhivāsam||7||

Until the feet of the Lord of Uma are revered

by mortals, they will not attain tranquillity and well-being in this life

or the hereafter, nor will they be liberated from suffering.

Please be gracious, O Lord who dwells within all beings. ||7||

न जानामि योगं जपं नैव पूजां

नतोऽहं सदा सर्वदा शम्भुतुभ्यम् ।

जराजन्मदुःखौघ तातप्यमानं

प्रभो पाहि आपन्नमामीश शंभो ॥८॥

na-jānami-yogam-japam-naiva-pujām

natoham-sadā-sarvadā-sambhu-tubhyam

jarā-janma-dukh-[a]ud-tātapya-mānam

prabho-pāahi-āapan-ma-misa-sambho||8||

(I offer my salutations to Bhagavan Shiva),

I am unfamiliar with yoga, mantras, or rituals of devotion.

Yet, I consistently bow before you, O Shambhu, at all times.

Please shield me from the agony of aging, the cycles of birth and death,

and from the burdens of sins that cause misery.

Grant me your protection, O Lord, and deliver me from all suffering, O Shambhu. ||8||

रुद्राष्टकमिदं प्रोक्तं विप्रेण हरतोषये

ये पठन्ति नरा भक्त्या तेषां शम्भुः प्रसीदति ॥९॥

rudrāshtakam-idam-proktam-viprena-hara-toshaye

ye-pathanti-narā-bhaktyā-teshām-shambhu-prasidati||9||

It is proclaimed by the wise that anyone who recites this Rudrashtakam

with devotion to honour Shiva will easily earn the favour of Shambhu. ||9||

Glossary of Confusing Terms and frequently used short forms

1.	PEP	Positive energy Particle – i.e. a point in space where 1 Planck Compartment or a volume of 1 Planck Volume of space is destroyed every one Planck Time. It is the smallest quantum of Positive Energy in DGR.
2.	NEP	Negative: energy Particle – i.e. a point in space where 1 Planck Compartment or a volume of 1 Planck Volume of space is created every one Planck Time. It is the smallest quantum of Negative Energy in DGR
3.	PEP aggregate	When PEPs interact with each other, they pull each other and form aggregates

4.	NEP lattice	When NEPs interact with a PEP aggregate, they repel each other and the PEP aggregate and form a lattice
5.	Universal time	Time running with constant speed everywhere in the Universe – Equivalent to time in Quantum Mechanics
6.	Local time	Time in DGR which all our instruments can measure which seems to vary depending on the status of contraction or expansion of space. It is also called as Variable time and is equivalent to time in General Relativity.
7.	Time dilation	In a place where Local time is dilated, there will be active spatial contraction happening either due to presence of PEPs or due to compensatory changes in the surrounding space
8.	Time contraction in DGR	In a place where Local time is contracted, there will be active spatial expansion either due to presence of NEPs or due to compensatory changes in the surrounding space

9.	PC aggregates	Aggregation of Planck compartments. They form to compensate for the PC void created due to the processes of destruction or creation. They are different than PEP aggregates.
10.	EPCAs	Eddy Planck compartment aggregates - One PC thick aggregates of PCs which are spherical in shape and are formed to compensate for the void created due to presence of excessive destruction or creation at a point
11.	Curved EPCAs	When local time varies significantly between neighbouring PC aggregates, the spatial contraction or expansion is variable, thus the EPCAs formed are curved.

12.	Straight EPCAs	When local time does not vary significantly between neighbouring PC aggregates, the spatial contraction or expansion is almost the same i.e. does not vary as we go from centre to periphery. Here, horizontal spatial contraction or expansion is negligible but horizontal spatial expansion or contraction keeps happening at a relatively constant acceleration as just shifting of the EPCAs. These are responsible for MONDian gravity as per DGR
13.	Push band	A narrow corridor of space with extreme time contraction i.e. spatial expansion to compensate for the excessive creation of space happening in the NEP lattice. They are responsible for repulsion between charges
14.	Pull band	A narrow corridor of space with extreme time dilation i.e. spatial contraction to compensate for the excessive destruction of space happening in the PEPs aggregated in the core. They are responsible for the attraction between charges

15.	Planck time	10^{-43} seconds
16.	Planck length	10^{-35} meters
17.	PC	The smallest indivisible portion of space equivalent to an atom of space. It is an assumption of DGR – A Planck Compartment
18.	PC vacuum	Whatever is present in between two PCs. This gives elasticity to space and leads to compensatory changes in space due any changes. It is an assumption of DGR
19.	QM	Quantum Mechanics
20.	GR	General Relativity
21.	DGR	Dynamic General Relativity
22.	VSL type of GR	Variable speed of light type of General Relativity
23.	MOND	Modified Newtonian Dynamics: A theory described by Mordehai Milgrom which says that at Galaxy scales, i.e. at extremely low accelerations due to gravity, Newtonian dynamics needs to be modified

24.	MONDian Gravity	Gravitational pull of a star beyond the Gravitational limit beyond which Newtonian dynamics stops being applicable and needs to be modified according to MOND. Beyond this, the Gravitational time dilation goes below significant level and Curved EPCAs are replaced by Straight EPCAs
25.	MONDian bonds	Diamond like bonds formed between peripheral stars due to Straight EPCAs. It is a prediction of DGR explaining high rotation velocities seen in the peripheral stars in a Galaxy
26.	DSE	Double slit experiment
27.	SE-DSE	Single electron Double slit experiment
28.	LQG	Loop Quantum gravity – one of the Theories of Quantum Gravity from which the assumption of "indivisible component of space called as the Planck Compartment is borrowed from

29.	Quantum foam	At extremely small scales, there exist minor fluctuations of energy in the form of spontaneously forming particle antiparticle pairs. These are virtual particles.
30.	Mach's principle	A principle probably described by Ernst Mach but named by Albert Einstein, which states that inertial forces (especially in the form of centrifugal forces in a rotating body like a rotating bucket full of water) originate due to the mass distribution of rest of the Universe.
31.	G	The Gravitational constant
32.	TRW	Time resetting waves

Sanskrit/Devnagari terms used in English with meanings

Aakash (आकाश) - Sky or space

Agni (अग्नी) - Fire

Agyan (अज्ञान) - Lack of knowledge

Agyani (अज्ञानी) - people who have less or no knowledge

Ahankara (अहंकार) or Aham (अहम्) - Ego or pride. Self-love or a tendency to overestimate ones Aja (अज) - the one who has no beginning i.e. no birth

Ajar (अजर) - the one who never gets old

Akhandam (अखण्डं) - i.e. fully complete all by himself,

Amar (अमर) - the one who has no end or cannot be destroyed

Anand (आनंद) - Happiness

Anant (अनंत) - With no end

Anaadi (अनादी) - With no beginning/birth

Apasmara Purusha (अपस्मार पुरुष) - an immortal demon that is subdued or suppressed by Shiva while performing Tandav dance in his Nataraja form. The demon represents ignorance especially, spiritual ignorance. Shiva being the embodiment of knowledge keeps suppressing it.

Ardhanarishwara (अर्धनारिष्वर) - the lord who is half male and half female. A representation that Shiva and Shakti are one and the same

Asur (असुर) - a demon, in the Puranic literature, people with predominance of Tamas.

Artha (अर्थ) - One of the four Goals of human life, it includes satisfaction achieved by getting wealth

Atma Shatakam (अत्मश्टकं) - Also called as Nirvanashatakam is a non-dualistic composition consisting of six verses written by Adi Shankaracharya in which the essence of Vedantic teaching is given. In it, an attempt is made to answer the question "Who am I" or "What am I" or rather "what I am Not". Most of these verses end with the verse "Shivoham" which means "I am Shiva" which essentially means Shiva is within us.

Avinashi (अविनाशी) - The one who cannot be destroyed

Bhagawan (भगवान) - God

Bhagavad Gita (भगवत गीता) - It is a group of Verses which is a part of the Mahabharata, a text written by Sage Ved Vyas. It is said to be direct word of God and was iterated by Lord Krishna to his friend and devotee Arjuna during the battle of Kurukshetra. It is considered the holiest text in Sanatan Dharma and all Sanatanis are supposed to read it, inculcate all wisdom within it and follow its advices.

Bhanukoti- prakasham (भानुकोटिप्रकाशं) i.e. has the effulgence of a million suns.

Bholenaath (भोलेनाथ) - The one who has no desire for "self-importance", one of the names of the Lord Shiva

Bramha (ब्रम्हा) - The Creator, one of the principal deities in Sanatan dharma, said to be the one responsible for the Creation of this Universe (Shristi)

Bramhalok (ब्रह्म लोक) - Adobe of Bramha

Budhi-daata (बुध्दिदाता) - The one who gives intelligence, the seat of intelligence

Chandrashekhar (चंद्रशेखर) - The one who has the crescent Moon on his forehead

Chaturbhuj (चतुर्भुज) - The one who has four hands. This is one of the many forms of Shri Hari Vishnu

Chit (चित्) - Consciousness

Chitt (चित्त) - The subconscious mind or the Mind

Chit- anand- sandoh (चिदानन्दसंदोह) - i.e. the one who gives eternal bliss

Damaru (डमरू): A small two headed drum like musical instrument, commonly having two long strings with beads attached to it. It is played by alternatingly rotating it so that the beads strike one side and then the other.

Devi (देवी) - Goddess

Dev (देव) - Gods

Dharma(धर्म) - One of the four Goals of human life, it includes long term satisfaction one achieves when one fulfils one's duties and

Fala (फल) - Consequences of action. They could be good or bad. Good deeds lead to Punya and bad deeds lead to Paap

Ganesha - The deity in Sanatan Dharma with an elephant's head. Son of Parvati and Lord Shiva.

Gangadhar (गंगाधर) - the one who holds the river Ganga in his matted hair, one of the names of Lord Shiva

Giragyanagoteetameesham (गिराज्ञानगोतीतमीशं) *i.e.* he cannot be described in words or speech,

Guna (गुण): Property or Characteristic

Halahal (हलाहल) or Kaal koot (काल कूट) - A poison that came out from the process of churning of the ocean

Jada (जड) - Not Conscious

Jal (जल) - Water

Jiva (जीव)- A living being, usually restricted to a conscious being especially human, In Sanatan dharma, it is different than a soul. It has a beginning and an end as is tied to the karmic cycles.

Kaal (काल) - time

Kalpantakari (कल्पान्तकारी) the one who ends a kalp i.e. a single cycle of creation and destruction of the Universe.

Kalp (कल्प) - a single cycle of creation and destruction of the Universe.

Kama (काम) - one of the four Goals of human life, it includes physical pleasures or short-term pleasures

Kama Deva (काम देव) - the god of desire or attraction especially sexual attraction towards the opposite sex and to have desire for a physical relation

Kamalnayan (कमलनयन) - The one with the eyes like a Lotus flower, one of the names of Shri Hari Vishnu

Kan Kan mein (कण कण में) - in every particle

Karma (कर्म) - Action or activity. Alternatively, it can be said as making a choice of what activity to do

Ketaki (केतकी) - a type of a shrub commonly found in India which has beautiful whitish yellow flower with multiple orderly placed petals. The flower is said to be disliked by Lord Shiva.

Kshirsaagar (क्षीरसागर): The ocean of milk, metaphorically probably the space in the early times of formation of the Universe when only radiation was present

Krishna: The one who is greyish black in colour, one of the avatars of Shri Hari Vishnu

Lakshmi (लक्ष्मी) - The deity in Sanatan Dharma who is represents Wealth and Beauty, Consort of Shri Hari Vishnu

Lobh (लोभ) - greed

Manmathari (मन्मथारी) - i.e. the one who killed Kama Deva, the God of desire

Mahakaal (महाकाल) - the one who is the master of Time or the one who controls the time or alternatively the one who is time itself.

Maya (माया) - Deception or Illusion

Mad (मद) - pride or ego or ahankar

Matsara (मत्सर) - Jealosy or feeling of hatred because of having less than others

Mithya (मिथ्या) - Unreal

Moksha (मोक्ष) - the Ultimate goal of all the souls in Sanatan Dharma, the liberation from cycles of birth and death, the state of ultimate happiness, being united with the Parabrahma.,

Mohapahari (मोहापहारी) - i.e. the one who removes worldly entanglements

Moh (मोह) - Attachment or uncontrollable need for having something

Naad (नाद)- the alternating rhythmical sounds coming out from a Damru when the beads alternatingly strike the two sides of the drum

Narayan (नारायण) - One of the names of Shri Hari Vishnu

Nataraaj (नटराज) - the king of all artists, another name of Lord Shiva

Nateshwar (नटेश्वर) - The lord of actors, one of the names of Shiva

Neelkanth (नीलकंठ) - The one who has a blue neck, one of the names of Lord Shiva after his neck (throat) were discoloured after consuming the poison named Halaahal.

Nirgun (निर्गुण) - Formless

Nirvana-roopam (निर्वाणरूपं) - i.e. the giver of Nirvana or Moksha or ultimate bliss

Omkar (ओंकार) - Om is a sacred symbol and a sacred chant or mantra in Sanatan Dharma and represents the omnipresent and eternal nature of Shiva himself. One of the names of Lord Shiva is Omkareshwara. Om is also the sound of cosmic vibration.

Padmanabha (पद्मनाभ) - The one with a lotus sprouting through his Umbilicus, one of the names of Shri Hari Vishnu

Pancha Mahabhootas (पंचमहाभूत) - the five sacred elements that come together to form our body

Pataal (पाताल) - there are various meanings depending on context. It may mean a realm underneath the Earth where the Asuras live. An alternative meaning is the realm of the small i.e. microworld.

Parabrahma (परब्रम्ह) or Brahman (ब्रह्म) - The single deity who is - equivalent to Bramha, Vishnu and Mahesha. The omnipresent omniscient superhuman being that is primary reason for existence of everything and is the primary force behind all the change

Parameshwar (परमेश्वर) - The ultimate god

Paresham (परेशं) - i.e. all powerful (deity/parameshwara).

Parvati (पार्वती)- The consort of Lord Shiva

Patanjali Yoga sutras (पतंजली योगसूत्र) - A collection of Sanskrit on the Theory and practice of Yoga, it is one of the prominent works among Puranic literature which describes the functioning of the mind and the ways to keep the mind under control. The Sanskar Vritti Sanskar cycle is described in it.

Purusha (पुरुष) - Male form, alternatively Shiva or the one who is not

Prakriti (प्रकृती) - the Female form, alternatively Shakti or Adishakti or the one who is the better half of Shiva.

Prachandam (प्रचण्डं) - enormous in size

Prakrushtam (प्रकृष्टं) - i.e. superior to all,

Pragalbham (प्रगल्भं) - i.e. eternal unborn

Prithvi (पृथ्वी)- The Earth

Purusharthas (**पुरुषार्थ**) - The four Goals of human life (Dharma, Artha, Kama and Moksha)

Purari (पुरारी) - i.e. enemy of the demons named Tripurasuras

Ram Raksha Stotra (राम रक्षा स्तोत्र) - This is a Stotra (collection of verses) written by Sage Budhakaushika which describes all the various attributes of Shree Ram (an avatar of Shri Hari Vishnu) and includes prayer to seek protection

Rajasic (राजसिक) - the one who has a predominance of Rajo guna

Rajoguna (रजोगुण) or Rajas (रजस्) - It represents activity, over-enthusiasm, overexcitability or anxiousness. The people with a predominance of this guna have excessive attachment with worldly things, greed, excessive drive, jealousy, perfectionism, self-love, narcissism, over inflated ego, not thinking for the benefit of others, hatred, racism, doubtfulness regarding ability or intention of others.

Rudraksha (रुद्राक्ष) - the exact meaning is Rudra (Shiva) + Aksha (tears of) i.e. Tears of Lord Shiva. But mostly, they are small spherical irregular blackish brown dried seeds of a plant botanically called as Elaeocarpus ganitrus.

Sagun (सगुण) - The one who has some form (opposite of formless) alternatively it means with some definable properties or characteristics or the one which is bound by the three Gunas.

Sajjan (सज्जन) - Good people, righteous people i.e. those who follow the teachings of Vedas, Dharmic individuals

Sajjan-anand-data - (सज्जनानन्ददाता) - the one who gives happiness to the good people

Samudra Manthan (समुद्र मंथन) - the process of Churning of the ocean

Samudra (समुद्र) -the sea

Shiva (शिव) - The God of Destruction

Sarvlokaiknatham (सर्वलोकैकनाथम्) - the owner of the three realms, one of the names of Shri Hari Vishnu

Sanskar (संस्कार) - this is a unique word in Vedic Literature with paucity of exact synonyms in English. It vaguely means Habit. It can also mean a Ritual (Antim Sanskar means Cremation). In Patanjali Yog sutras, Sanskar is a type of programming of the mind which determines what impulses or Vritti one might get in the future. These Sanskars are supposed to be stored in the Subconsious mind and come back into the Conscious mind at a later date as Vritti.

Saraswati (सरस्वती) - The deity in Sanatan Dharma who represents Knowledge and Learning, Consort of Lord Bramha

Sarva Vyapi (सर्वव्यापी) - the one who is omnipresent or who encompasses everything or is present everywhere

Sat (सत्) - Truth

Sattvaguna (सत्वगुण) or Satva (सत्व) - It is best of the three Gunas. It represents all the positive things like goodness, empathy, kindness, peace, good behaviour, unity, renunciation, lack of attachment, a limit to one's desires, no jealousy, no greed, an innate ability to help others or do philanthropy.

Sattvic (सात्विक) - the one who has a predominance of Sattva guna

Srishti (सृष्टी) - the Universe

Shakti (शक्ती) - literally means Energy or strength, alternatively in this context, the Female deity, the mother of all, Goddess Aadishakti

Shada Ripu (शड रिपु) - the six enemies of the mind, they are kama i.e. desire, krodh i.e. anger, moh i.e. greed or attachment, mad i.e. ego or pride or ahankara and matsar i.e. jealousy.

Shiva (शिव) - The Destroyer, one of the principal deities in Sanatan dharma, said to be the one responsible for carrying out destruction of this Universe (Shristi) to maintain balance against Creation

Sudarshan Chakra (सुदर्शन चक्र): A rotating disclike weapon which is the primary weapon of Shri Hari Vishnu

Shankh(शंख): Conch

Sheshnaag (शेषनाग): The Multiheaded snake on which Vishnu resides

Shyam (श्याम): The one who is greyish black in colour, one of the names of Shri Hari Vishnu

Sthitapradnya (स्थितप्रज्ञ)- A state of self in which a person isn't too happy on success or occasion of happiness and not too sad due to failure or a sad event in life. Such people have their emotions under control and can thus control what emotions control them and which don't. An inexact synonym is emotional intelligence.

Tamasic (तामसिक) - the one who has a predominance of Tamo Guna

Tamoguna (तमोगुण) or Tamas (तमस्) - It represents darkness or lack of knowledge. People with a predominance of Tamas have poor knowledge, are unable to understand right from wrong or good from bad, are lazy, jealous, excessively angry, rude, tendency to complain all the time, poor levels of satisfaction, tendency to fight, tendency to focus on negativity.

Tandav (तांडव) - The divine dance done by Shiva

Trideva (त्रिदेव) - the three principal deities in Sanatan Dharma

Trishul (त्रिशूल) - The trident. A weapon commonly seen with Shiva

Trilokadhipati (त्रिलोकनाथ) - the one who is the owner or master of the three realms, one of the names of Shri Hari Vishnu

Triloknath - the owner of the three realms, one of the names of Shri Hari Vishnu/ Shiva

Trigunatmak (त्रिगुणात्मक): Having three properties

Trigunateet (त्रिगुणातीत): The one who has mastery or control over all the three Gunas or properties

Tripurasuras (त्रिपुरासूर) - name of three Asurs who went against the teachings of Vedas.

Vasuki (वासुकी) - The snake on the Neck of Lord Shiva

Vedas (वेद)- Sacred Scriptures of Sanatan Dharma

Vishnu Sahastranaam (विष्णू सहस्त्रनाम) - the thousand names of Vishnu

Vishnu (विष्णू) - The Preserver - one of the principal deities in Sanatan dharma, said to be the one responsible for preservation of this Universe (Shristi)

Vaikunth (वैकुंठ) or Vishnulok (विष्णू लोक) - Adobe of Vishnu

Vayu (वायू) - the wind or air

Vinashi (विनाशी) - The one who can be destroyed

Vinayaka (विनायक) - The God of Wisdom, Son of Shiva and Parvati, another name for Ganesh

Vishwaroop (विष्वरूप): It is a form of Vishnu in described in the Bhagavad Gita in which he has thousands of heads, thousands of mouths and thousands of arms. He is the one who gives birth, he is the one who nurtures and he is also the one who causes death, he is one and only single deity I.e. all deities are different forms of Shri Hari Vishnu and there is no difference between the Trideva.

Vibhuti (विभूती) - the sacred Ash

Vritti (वृत्ती) - An impulse. A sudden urge to do a particular activity or feeling of need to do an activity. In Patanjali Yogasutras and also in the Bhagwad Gita, the Mind puts impulses or vritti in the consciousness which can either be approved or dis-approved by the conscious mind.

Yuga (युग) - A long period of time, probably thousands of years, in Vedic and Puranic literature there are four Yugas, Satya yuga, Treta yuga, Dwapar yuga and Kali yuga.

Sanskrit to English notations

ā - आ i.e. extended version similar to “aa”

ī - ई i.e. extended version similar to “ii” or “ee”

ū- ऊ i.e. extended version similar to “uu” or “oo”

ñ- ण

ś /*ś*- श i.e. “sh”

ṁ- म् i.e. half version of म which is often used in Sanskrit

Coloured Images

Coloured Image 1: Kshirsagar – the metaphorical Ocean of Milk, the abode of Shri Hari Vishnu

Coloured Image 2: A brass idol of Vishnu lying down on a multi headed snake with a lotus blooming out from his umbilicus with Bramha within it and Shiva lingam by his side.

Coloured Image 3: Common depiction of Vishnu lying on a multiheaded snake Sheshnaag, floating in the ocean of milk with Bramha within a lotus arising from umbilicus of Vishnu and Laxmi by the side. Not shown here is the Shiva lingam commonly shown by the side of Vishnu

Coloured image 4: Shows the Ardhanarishwara form of Shiva wherein Prakriti or Parvati is shown as an integral part of Shiva and is left half of Shiva

Coloured image 5: Shows Shiva as commonly described in the Vedas. He has snakes around his neck, wears a tiger skin with stripes, has a trident, has a damru, has the river Ganga flowing out of his matted hair, has ornaments made up of Rudraksh and has a crescent moon on his forehead. Note the three eyes (Trilochana) and the blue hued throat (Neelakanth). Also note the eternal Bliss radiating from his face and the posture of

giving boon suggesting that he is the giver of happiness and giver of boons for the upliftment of everyone.

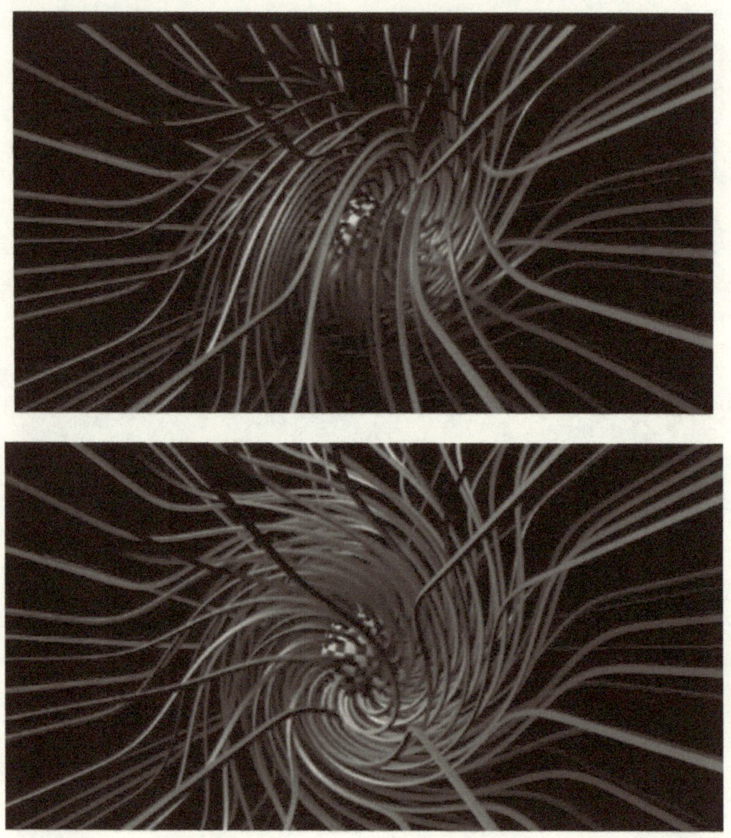

Coloured image 6: Shows a diagrammatic representation of the Spinor model with a central sphere with thread-like connections spiralling around it extending outwards towards infinity. (Image Courtesy: Wikipedia)

Coloured image 7: Shiva's Rudraksha

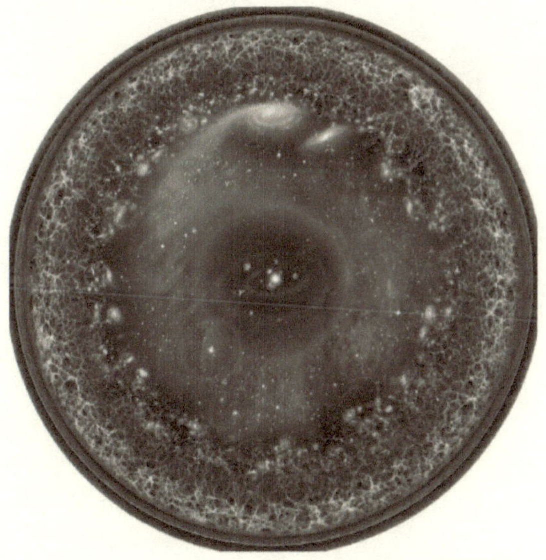

Coloured image 8: Entire Universe in one frame
(as if it is within a single Rudraksh of Shiva)

www.ingramcontent.com/pod-product-compliance
Lightning Source LLC
LaVergne TN
LVHW041152150826
845673LV00001B/136